About ApressOpen

What Is ApressOpen?

- ApressOpen is an open access book program that publishes high-quality technical and business information.

- ApressOpen eBooks are available for global, free, noncommercial use.

- ApressOpen eBooks are available in PDF, ePub, and Mobi formats.

- The user friendly ApressOpen free eBook license is presented on the copyright page of this book.

To Gautama Buddha, whose teachings inspired me to explore a more nature based approach to edge networking as described in this book.

Rethinking the Internet of Things

A Scalable Approach to Connecting Everything

Francis daCosta

Apress
open

Rethinking the Internet of Things: A Scalable Approach to Connecting Everything

Francis daCosta

ISBN-13 (pbk): 978-1-4302-5740-0

ISBN-13 (electronic): 978-1-4302-5741-7

President and Publisher: Paul Manning
Lead Editor: Jeffrey Pepper
Project Manager: Byron Henderson
Technical Editor: John Aiken
Coordinating Editor: Jill Balzano
Cover Designer: Anna Ishchenko

Distributed to the book trade worldwide by Springer Science+Business Media New York, 233 Spring Street, 6th Floor, New York, NY 10013. Phone 1-800-SPRINGER, fax (201) 348-4505, e-mail orders-ny@springer-sbm.com, or visit www.springeronline.com.

For information on translations, please e-mail rights@apress.com, or visit www.apress.com.

Contents at a Glance

Contents

About the Author

Francis daCosta founded and acted as CTO for MeshDynamics (wireless mesh networking), Advanced Cybernetics Group (embedded software for robot control systems and other mission-critical military applications), and Knowmadic (web-based big data extraction). Previously, he served as an adviser to the United States Air Force Robotics and Automation Center of Excellence (RACE). He also held senior technical positions at MITRE, Northrop Grumman, Ingersoll-Rand, and Xerox. His entrepreneurial projects have also included autonomous robotic systems and adaptive process controllers.

Mr. daCosta has a MS from Stanford University and a BS from the Indian Institute of Technology, along with post-graduate work in artificial intelligence at the University of California, Los Angeles. He is currently involved in a stealth-mode Internet of Things start-up and has authored or co-authored 15 patents incorporating a variety of technology innovations including adaptive control, self-healing mesh networks, sensor fusion, machine learning, distributed control, and automatic robot programming. His intellectual interests include machine intelligence, subsumption architectures, emergence, and consilience.

About the Project Manager

Byron Henderson has been working in data communications and networking for thirty years in a variety of marketing, product management, sales, and general management roles. Companies have included MeshDynamics, Cisco Systems, Stratacom, Fibermux (later ADC Telecommunications), MICOM Systems (later Nortel Networks), and ComDesign (later Network Equipment Technologies). His areas of technology focus have included wireless networking, voice-over-IP, routing and switching, security, and more. Before discovering that communications offered a better career path than crustaceans, he studied aquatic biology at the University of California, Santa Barbara.

About the Technical Reviewer

John Aiken took his BSEE at Cornell University. He worked in silicon fabrication process engineering in implant, diffusion and thin films for several chip companies. John moved into development, as a founder of one of the first companies providing low cost, high performance satellite television receivers to the consumer market. He developed high reliability power avionics for the defense and space sectors, designed broadcast video-graphics systems and managed development of pioneering graphics supercomputers for space shuttle flight simulation at NASA Johnson Space Center. Working at Lockheed Martin, John provided software and systems engineering expertise in the communications, navigation and training markets. He developed protocols for networked simulation and performed operations planning for the Air Force Satellite Control Network. At Intel, John managed development of software for server applications and developed specifications for open communications systems.

Working in global telecommunications standards, John managed development of requirements, architectures, protocols and interoperability testing for 4G mobile networks and devices.

Recently John has done business process re-engineering for the utility industry. He has aided in the development of technical educational infrastructure and is facilitating the advancement of initiatives in network, software tools and in the architecture of the Internet of Things.

John invented, patented and licensed key display and image processing technologies for the smartphone and tablet computer markets. He has held certification as a Project Management Professional since 2003.

Acknowledgments

Writing a book like this has been a journey through my past and planned future endeavors. I am indebted to my many clients and collaborators through the years at the MITRE Corporation, National Institute of Standards and Technology, Department of Energy, United States Navy, and the United States Air Force, all of whom involved me in projects that explored the cutting edge in embedded systems, control systems, and robotics. The support and suggestions of customers of MeshDynamics, Inc. helped refine many of the networking ideas that I have built upon for this book.

John Aiken of Intel Corporation offered key encouragement and insight in getting this project started, and Jeffrey Pepper of Apress has been a knowledgeable and patient guide through the sometimes-arcane book publishing process. The book would not have been started without John – and wouldn't have been finished without Jeffrey!

Alok Batra has been a sounding board for many of the ideas developed in this book and was a gracious contributor of the Foreword.

Managing Editor Byron Henderson has been a valued colleague for years and helped me to turn dense technical details into more readable prose while offering ideas and suggestions to improve the final result. His knowledge of and enthusiasm for the biological principles of massive natural systems informed many of the concepts in this book.

All of these, and many more unnamed, contributed to the completion of this book, but any errors that remain are my own.

Foreword

With the rise of machines talking with machines in the Internet of Things, a new category of applications will demand evolutionary changes in the infrastructure of networks. Traditional networks were built to keep the enterprise at the center, resulting in star topologies and round-trip communications from edge devices to the servers at the center of the network. The Internet was similarly designed around information at the center of the network connected to people at the edges.

But machines are different from people, with different communications needs. Machines operate more independently in real-time and their actions affect the physical world immediately. Feedback and control of these local actions is critical for top performance and safety. Unlike the traditional end-to-end Internet, the Internet of Things must address these deterministic local control loops to insure business process reliability.

The different needs of machine communications can be seen in three aspects: real-time response, deterministic performance, and security and safety. All three aspects make demands on networking – closed control loops near the machines (to reduce latency), reduced costs of data transmission (in light of the rapidly expanding population of machines), and segregation of communications (to reduce noise and increase security).

With the increased number of devices and variety of applications, Metcalfe's Law is exploding with the number of new machines and the amount of data they generate. The only way for technology to keep up with the coming expansion of the Internet of Things is to manage the machine data flows differently from the way human application-oriented traffic has been handled with current protocols.

This book describes a critical new approach for the Internet of Things that makes it possible to extract meaning in context from the billions of new data sources that will emerge. This new approach recognizes the different demands of machine-to-machine networks and proposes an evolutionary three-tiered architecture to enable the next phase of the Internet.

Francis daCosta is distinctively qualified to develop this new IoT architecture. His diverse background in autonomous robotics, embedded systems, big data analysis, and wireless networking places him at the center of the all of the different technologies which must combine to address the Internet of Things. When Francis talks about communications realms, segregation of data streams, determinism, security, and control loops, I know that he is taking an innovative and disruptive approach in the evolutionary world of networks. This new architecture provides the urgently needed tools to address the expanding needs of the machines that join the physical world to the digital world in the Internet of Things.

Alok Batra
CEO, MQIdentity, Inc.
Former CTO & Chief Architect, GE Global Software Center, Industrial Internet Platform

Introduction

I didn't set out to develop a new architecture for the Internet of Things (IoT). Rather, I was thinking about the implications of control and scheduling within machine social networks in the context of Metcalfe's Law. The coming tsunami of machine-to-machine interconnections could yield tremendous flows of information – and knowledge.

Once we free the machine social network (comprised of sensors and an unimaginable number of other devices) from the drag of human interaction, there is tremendous potential for creating autonomous communities of machines that require only occasional interaction with, or reporting to, humans.

The conventional wisdom is that the expansive address space of IPv6 solves the IoT problem of myriad end devices. But the host-to-host assumptions fossilized into the IP protocol in the 1970s fundamentally limited its utility for the very edge of the IoT network. As the Internet of Things expands exponentially over the coming years, it will be expected to connect to devices that are cheaper, dumber, and more diverse. Traditional networking thinking will fail for multiple reasons.

First, although IPv6 provides an address for these devices, the largest population of these appliances, sensors, and actuators will lack the horsepower in terms of processors, memory, and bandwidth to run the bloated IP protocol stack. It simply does not make financial sense to burden a simple sensor with all of the protocol overhead needed for host-to-host communications.

Second, the conventional implementation of IP protocols implies networking knowledge on the part of device manufacturers: without centrally authorized MAC IDs and end-to-end management, IP falls flat. Many of the hundreds of thousands of manufacturers of all sizes worldwide building moisture sensors, streetlights, and toasters lack the technical expertise to implement legacy network technology in traditional ways.

Third, the data needs of the IoT are completely different from the global Internet. Most of the communications will be terse machine-to-machine interchanges that are largely asymmetrical, with much more data flowing in one direction (sensor to server, for example) than in the other. And in most cases, losing an individual message to an intermittent or noisy connection will be no big deal. Unlike the traditional Internet, which is primarily human-oriented (and thus averse to data loss), much of the Internet of Things traffic will be analyzed over time, not acted upon immediately. Most of the end devices will be essentially autonomous, operating independently whether anyone is "listening" or not.

Fourth, when there are real-time sensing and response loops needed in the Internet of Things, traditional network architectures with their round-trip control loops will be problematic. Instead, a way would be needed to engender independent local control loops managing the "business" of appliances, sensors, and actuators while still permitting occasional "advise and consent" communications with central servers.

Finally, and most importantly, traditional IP peer-to-peer relationships lock out much of the potential richness of the Internet of Things. There will be vast streams of data flowing, many of which are unknown or unplanned. Only a publish/subscribe architecture allows us to tap into this knowledge by discovering interesting data flows and relationships. And only a publish/subscribe network can scale to the tremendous size of the coming Internet of Things.

The only systems on earth that have ever scaled to the size and scope of the Internet things are natural systems: pollen distribution, ant colonies, redwoods, and so on. From examining these natural systems, I developed the concept of a three-tiered IoT architecture described in this book: simple end devices; networking specialist propagator nodes, and information-seeking integrator functions. In these pages, I'll explain why terse, self-classified messages, networking overhead isolated to a specialized tier of devices, and the publish/subscribe relationships formed are the only way to fully distill the power of the coming Internet of Things.

Francis daCosta
Santa Clara, California, 2013

■ ■ ■

CHAPTER 1

It's Different Out Here

The emergence of the Internet of Things (IoT) destroys every precedent and preconceived notion of network architecture. To date, networks have been invented by engineers skilled in protocols and routing theory. But the architecture of the Internet of Things will rely much more upon lessons derived from nature than traditional (and ossified, in my opinion) networking schemes. This chapter will consider the reasons why the architecture for the Internet of Things must incorporate a fundamentally different architecture from the traditional Internet, explore the technical and economic foundations of this new architecture, and finally begin to outline a solution to the problem.

Why the Internet of Things Requires a New Solution

The architecture of the original Internet was created long before communicating with billions of very simple devices such as sensors and appliances was ever envisioned. The coming explosion of these much simpler devices creates tremendous challenges for the current networking paradigm in terms of the number of devices, unprecedented demands for low-cost connectivity, and impossibility of managing far-flung and diverse equipment. Although these challenges are becoming evident now, they will pose a greater, more severe problem as this revolution accelerates. This book describes a new paradigm for the Internet of Things; but first, the problem.

It's Networking on the Frontier

The IoT architecture requires a much more organic approach compared with traditional networking because it represents an extreme frontier in communications. The scope and breadth of the devices to be connected are huge, and the connections to the edges of the network where these devices will be arrayed will be "low fidelity": low-speed, lossy (where attenuation and interference may cause lost but generally insignificant data, as depicted in Figure 1-1), and intermittent. At the same time, much of the communication will be machine-to-machine and in tiny snatches of data, which is completely the *opposite* of networks such as the traditional Internet.

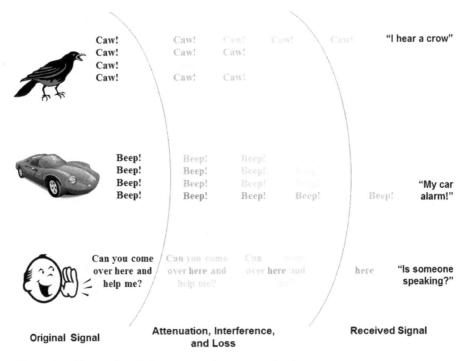

Figure 1-1. *The results of a lossy connection at an end point*

Exploring the characteristics of the traditional Internet highlights the very different requirements for the frontier of the emerging Internet of Things. Conventionally, data networks have been over-provisioned; that is, built with more capacity than is typically required for the amount of information to be carried. Even the nominally "best effort" traditional Internet is massively over-provisioned in many aspects. If it weren't, the Internet couldn't work: protocols such as TCP/IP are fundamentally based on a *mostly* reliable connection between sender and receiver.

Because Moore's Law provided a "safety valve" in the form of ever-increasing processor speeds and memory capacities, even the explosive growth of the Internet over the last two decades has not exceeded the capabilities of devices such as routers, switches, and PCs, in part because they are continually replaced at 3- to 5-year intervals with devices with more memory and processing power.

These devices are inherently multipurpose: they are designed with software, hardware, and (often) human access and controls. What is important about this point is that the addition of networking capability, usually in the form of protocol "stacks," is nearly free. The processor power, memory, and so on already exist as byproducts of the devices' prime functions.

But the vast majority of devices to be connected in the coming IoT are very different. They will be moisture sensors, valve controls, "smart dust," parking meters, home appliances, and so on. These types of end devices almost *never* contain the processors, memory, hard drives, and other features needed to run a protocol stack.

These components are not necessary for the end devices' prime function, and the costs of provisioning them with these features would be prohibitive, or at least high enough to exclude wide use of many applications that could otherwise be well served. So these simpler devices are very much "on their own" at the frontier of the network.

Today's Internet doesn't reach this frontier; it simply isn't cost-effective to do so, as will be explored later. Thus, it isn't possible to overprovision in the same way networks have traditionally been built. On the frontier, devices in every aspect should therefore be more self-sufficient, from their naming, to protocols, to security. There simply isn't the "safety net" of device performance, over-provisioning, a defined end-to-end connection, and management infrastructure as in traditional networking.

It Will be (Even) Bigger than Expected

As a growing number of observers realize, one of the most important aspects of the emerging Internet of Things is its incredible breadth and scope. Within a few years, devices on the IoT will vastly outnumber human beings on the planet—and the number of devices will continue to grow. Billions of devices worldwide will form a network unprecedented in history. Devices as varied as soil moisture sensors, street lights, diesel generators, video surveillance systems—even the legendary Internet-enabled toasters—will all be connected in one fashion or another. See Figure 1-2 for some examples.

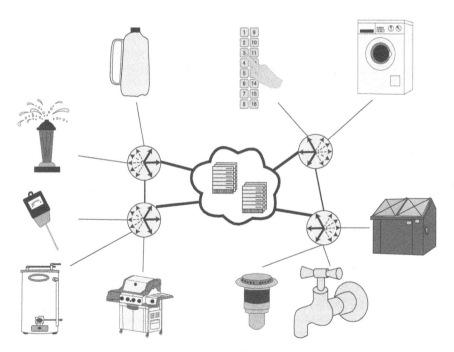

Figure 1-2. *A wide variety of end devices will be connected to the Internet of Things*

Some pundits have focused only on the myriad addresses necessary for the sheer arithmetic count of devices and have pronounced IPv6 sufficient for the IoT. But this mistakes *address space* for *addressability*. No central address repository or existing address translation scheme can possibly deal with the frontier aspects of the IoT. Nor can addresses alone create the costly needed networking "horsepower" within the appliances, sensors, and actuators.

Devices from millions of manufacturers based in hundreds of countries will appear on the IoT (and disappear) completely unpredictably. This creates one of the greatest challenges of the IoT: management. This is a matter both of scope and device capabilities.

Consider smartphones, for example, which are expected to become the most common computing and communications platforms in the world. This number has recently been placed at 1.4 billion, or roughly one for every five persons on the planet. A similar figure has been estimated for PCs, bringing the total worldwide for these two types of devices to about 3 billion.

These devices incorporate the processors, memory, and human interfaces necessary for traditional networking protocol stacks (typically IPv6 today), the human interfaces necessary for control, and an infrastructure for management (unique addresses, management servers, and so on). The prices (and profit margins) of these devices mean that it is cost-effective for manufacturers (and governments) to keep track of addresses, feature sets, software revisions, and so on.

But the situation for the actuators, sensors, and appliances of the Internet of Things is vastly different. Considering the number of appliances per citizen in developed countries alone, the number is staggering: each of these individuals probably makes use of dozens of these devices each day. Even residents of *developing* countries interact with multiple end devices and sensors daily—and those numbers are growing with rising standards of living. Add to that a vast array of traffic-light controls, security devices, and status sensors operated by various levels of government, and the number of potential IoT end devices rapidly grows to a couple of orders of magnitude greater than the world's population (7 billion and counting, as of this writing).

The estimated 700 billion IoT devices (see Figure 1-3) cannot be individually managed; they can only be accommodated. It will simply not be possible to administer the addressing of this huge population of communicating machines through traditional means such as IPv6 *nor will it be necessary to do so*. Instead, self-addressing and self-classification will provide the answers, as explained in Chapter 3.

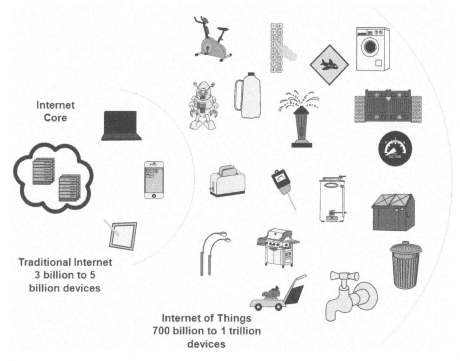

Figure 1-3. *The quantity of devices in the Internet of Things will dwarf the traditional Internet and thus cannot be networked with current protocols, tools, and techniques*

Terse, Purposeful, and Uncritical

The kinds of information these hundreds of billions of IoT devices exchange will also be very different from the traditional Internet—at least the Internet we've known since the 1990s. Much of today's Internet traffic is primarily human-to-machine oriented. Applications such as e-mail, web browsing, and video streaming consist of relatively large chunks of data generated by machines and consumed by humans. As such, they tend to be asymmetrical and bursty in data flows, with a relatively large amount of data exchanged in each "session" or "conversation."

But the typical IoT data flow will be nearly diametrically opposed to this model. Machine-to-machine communications require minimal packaging and presentation overhead. For example, a moisture sensor in a farmer's field may have only a single value to send of volumetric water content. It can be communicated in a few characters of data, perhaps with the addition of a location/identification tag. This value might change slowly throughout the day, but the frequency of *meaningful* updates will be low. Similar terse communication forms can be imagined for millions of other types of IoT sensors and devices. Many of these IoT devices may be simplex or nearly simplex in data flows, simply broadcasting a state or reading over and over while switched on without even the capacity to "listen" for a reply.

This raises another aspect of the typical IoT message: it's individually *unimportant*. For simple sensors and state machines, the variations in conditions over time may be small. Thus, any individual transmission from the majority of IoT devices is likely completely uncritical. These messages are being collected and interpreted elsewhere in the network, and a gap in data will simply be ignored or extrapolated (see Figure 1-4).

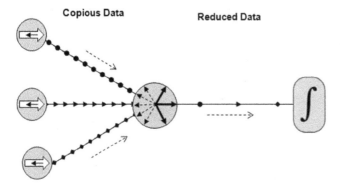

Figure 1-4. *Multiple identical messages may be received; some are discarded*

Even more complex devices, such as a remotely monitored diesel generator, should generate little more traffic, again in terse formats unintelligible to humans, but gathered and interpreted by other devices in the IoT. Overall, the *meaningful* amount of data generated from each IoT device is vanishingly small—nearly exactly the opposite of the trends seen in the traditional Internet. For example, a temperature sensor might generate only a few hundred bytes of useful data per day, about the same as a couple of smartphone text messages. Because of this, very low bandwidth connections might be utilized for savings in cost, battery life, and other factors. On the IoT frontier, just as in the mythical "Old West," laconic characters will be appreciated.

Dealing with Loss

Today's traditional Internet is extremely reliable, even if labeled "best effort." Over-provisioning of bandwidth (for normal situations) and backbone routing diversity have created an expectation of high service levels among Internet users. "Cloud" architectures and the structure of modern business organizations are built on this expectation of Internet quality and reliability.

But at the extreme edges of the network that will make up the *vast statistical majority of the IoT*, connections may often be intermittent and inconsistent in quality. Devices may be switched off at times or powered by solar cells with limited battery back-up. Wireless connections may be of low bandwidth or shared among multiple devices.

Traditional protocols such as TCP/IP are designed to deal with lossy and inconsistent connections by resending data. Even though the data flowing to or from any individual IoT device may be exceedingly small, it will grow quite large in aggregate IoT traffic. The inefficiencies of resending vast quantities of *mostly individually unimportant* data are clearly an unnecessary redundancy. Again, recall that for the vast majority of IoT devices, a lost message (or even a substantial string of messages) is not meaningful. (For those devices that are sending or receiving timely mission-critical information, traditional Internet protocols are likely a better fit than the emerging IoT architecture.)

The Protocol Trap

It's extremely tempting to suggest existing widely deployed protocols such as TCP/IP for the IoT (see the sidebar " Why not IP for the IoT?" in Chapter 2). After all, they have already been engineered and are widely available in protocol stacks on billions of devices such as PCs and smartphones. But, as briefly noted, most of these protocols are ill-suited for many of the end devices with potential interest for the IoT.

The basic problem is the very robustness of these protocols. They are intrinsically designed for high-duty cycles, large data streams, and reliability. Each of these otherwise desirable characteristics is a poor fit for the IoT, as noted previously. But what's the harm, one might ask? Isn't more capability a good thing? Not for the Internet of Things.

Mind the Overhead

A key reason why robust protocols aren't needed (or possible) for the IoT is the overhead they require and the minimal processing, memory, and communications capabilities of many very simple IoT devices. This may come as a shock to some IoT thinkers who envision an IP stack on every light post and refrigerator. But when the IoT is considered from the proper "end of the telescope"—from the *edge* of the network in—this immediately becomes impractical, for all the reasons noted previously. Instead, it makes sense to provide a new solution that can run side by side with existing IP–enabled end devices to efficiently manage the immense amount of data being generated by devices for which IP support is unnecessary and perhaps a liability.

Much of what has been written to date about the IoT assumes a sophisticated networking stack in every refrigerator, parking meter, and fluid valve, so this may be a difficult idea to abandon. But from the forgoing discussion, it's obvious that these devices won't need the decades of built-up network protocol detritus encoded in TCP/IP, for example. One must free his or her thinking from personal experiences and concepts of the networking of computers, smartphones (and, by definition, human users) to address the much simpler needs of the myriad devices at the edge of the IoT.

Burdening otherwise simple devices such as power line sensors and coffee makers with a full networking protocol stack would serve only to massively increase the cost and complexity of billions of these devices. A traditional networking protocol stack requires a processor, operating system, memory, and other functions. Even if consolidated within a single chip, the complexity, power draw, and cost of this computing power is an unnecessary expense in the IoT. These costs will be considered later in this chapter.

As noted previously, the vast majority of IoT devices have very basic needs of sending or receiving a miniscule amount of data. The physical requirements may likewise be very simple: an integrated chip containing only the minimal interfaces and a means of transmission or reception.

More Smarts, More Risk

Although it may seem counterintuitive, dumber devices are safer. If every IoT device has some sort of operating system and memory, it becomes a potential subject for hacking or inadvertent misconfiguration. The operating systems and protocol stacks also require updating and management. Providing security and upgrades on the scale of the IoT for a massive number of devices, built and installed by millions of different manufacturers and individuals, is simply an impossible task (see Figure 1-5).

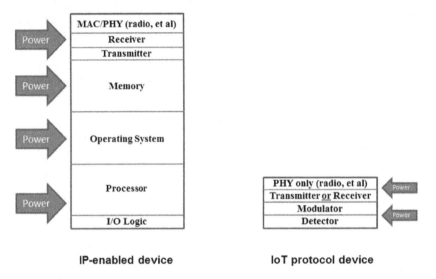

Figure 1-5. Contrasting the processor, OS, memory, and power necessary for traditional protocols vs. the IoT protocol

The Overhead of Overhead

Beyond the physical costs and management requirements, the *data* overhead of traditional networking is likewise overkill for the majority of the IoT. Traditional protocols are "sender-oriented"; that is, the sender must ensure that its message has been properly transmitted and received. This leads to extensive capabilities in terms of temporary storage of sent data, management of acknowledgments, and resending of lost or corrupted messages. And each of these robust capabilities is reflected in overhead data added to the message payload.

When this data overhead is considered in relation to the tiny snatches of data sent or received by the typical IoT device, the ratio of overhead to payload becomes ridiculous. Moreover, because each *individual* IoT message is completely *uncritical*, the check-and-retransmit overhead is an unnecessary expense in bandwidth and end device cost. It makes the most sense, therefore, for the emerging IoT architecture to be engineered for an absolute minimum of data overhead.

Humans Need Not Apply

Perhaps most importantly, traditional networking protocols and applications are almost all designed with the expectation of a human being on one end of the "conversation." These traditional approaches are inherently designed to communicate concepts and context for humans.

But the networking overhead associated with smooth streaming, echoing of typed characters, and intelligible presentation of data are completely unnecessary at the machine-to-machine device level in the Internet of Things. So a large percentage of the processing and data overhead of traditional protocols is totally redundant for the IoT. An architecture for the Internet of Things should provide only the minimal amount of overhead that is needed—and only at the point that it is needed—to maximize efficiency and minimize costs.

Economics and Technology of the Internet of Things

One of the great promises of bringing IPv6 to the traditional Internet was that it would provide all the address space needed to connect every device ever needed forever—including the Internet of Things, no matter how large it grew. And within that narrow definition, the promise is correct. Because of some quirks in the way that only part of the IPv6 address space has been released, the current theoretical number of hosts (communicating devices) on an IPv6 Internet is $3.4 \times 10^{*}38^{*}$.

This is indeed a huge number, which even the massive Internet of Things is unlikely to surpass. For this reason, many pundits and manufacturers (particularly those with a vested interest) have sanguinely said that IPv6 is already prepared for the Internet of Things. The world simply needs to keep doing what it has always done to incorporate the new IoT—there are more IP addresses available than grains of sand.

But this "head in the sand" approach ignores the key economic factor that will drive the deployment of the Internet of Things (as it has driven nearly every other networking technology): the cost at the end points. There are three broad areas where these costs accumulate and compel the need for a new approach in the Internet of Things: hardware and software, oversight and management, and security.

Functionality Costs Money

As noted earlier, traditional computing and communications devices such as PCs, tablets, and smartphones already incorporate processors, working memory, and storage in their design. These capabilities are necessary for their primary purpose. Adding IPv6 to these devices requires only the addition of a protocol stack that resides in storage, executes within working memory, and is powered by the processor.

Thus the incremental cost of adding IPv6 to these devices is indeed negligible, in fact barely measurable, when compared with the profit margins these devices generate. But these devices are *not a significant portion of the Internet of Things!* Numbering in the low billions today, their number will be dwarfed by the *hundreds of billions* of simple sensors and appliances in the IoT.

The vast majority of these simple end devices contain no processors, memory, or storage; and are not data-connected in any way today. This is a key point: the future of the Internet of Things is networking devices that have never been connected before. These devices are designed to be built and sold, for the most part, at the lowest cost yielding the highest margin. Those sold in developing countries, in particular, must be extremely inexpensive. Yet they are some of the very areas in which the IoT will grow most quickly. To capitalize on the enormous potential of the IoT, creating a standard low-cost solution will enable billions of devices that would otherwise continue to be off the grid, never developed, or added to the massive quantity of one-off solutions that are being spawned even today.

Inexpensive Devices Can't Bear Traditional Protocols

With a clearer picture of these cost realities in mind, it is immediately obvious that burdening moisture sensors, light bulbs, and the proverbial toaster with the additional hardware and software (not necessary for the basic functions of these sensors and appliances) needed to run traditional protocols such as IPv6 is a show-stopper. It has been estimated that the incremental cost of adding IPv6 to devices can be as much as $50, even in large quantities. (Note that beyond the processors and memory devices, additional Wi-Fi or Ethernet components are needed, and more power and heat dissipation will also be required).

Fortunately for the expansion of the Internet of Things, these simple devices do not require anything approaching the level of complexity offered by IPv6. Instead, simple modulation, broadcast, and receiving technologies will suffice, even including non-radio-frequency solutions such as infrared and power line networking. Assuming integration into silicon packages, costs for adding simple IoT networking (described in Chapter 2) to sensors and appliances will quickly approach $1 or less. The key is that this is barely "networking" in the traditional sense: broadcasting a state or receiving a simple instruction with no error correction, routing, or any other traditional networking functions. IoT devices are "dumb" in general, but they are exceedingly well-suited to a narrow task. At a very base level, it is easy to see that this cost argument alone is proof that the costs and the effort in creating a new solution for IoT devices are absolutely necessary. The result in not doing so would be that many of these new technologies and innovations would largely not come to pass. Others would be implemented at a cost that limits their usefulness. At what cost to growth, development, and prosperity?

And as noted previously, traditional one-size-fits-all networking protocols such as IPv6 burden even the smallest payloads with 1,000 bytes of data. In today's over-provisioned world, these wasted bytes are unnoticed. But when extrapolated to hundreds of billions of simple end devices sending and receiving hundreds of thousands of times each day, the potential for network congestion and huge expenditures by carriers is significant. New carrier build-outs to support the "plain vanilla" data networking of the IoT will be difficult to cost-justify.

Overseeing 700 Billion Devices

The count of manufacturers building networking equipment likely numbers in the millions. They are relatively easy to find and track because each traditional piece of networking equipment is associated with a MAC ID (Media Access Control Identification) assigned to the manufacturer. A large number, but there is a central database of manufacturers that is maintained by the IEEE (Institute of Electrical and Electronics Engineers).

For those manufacturers who are today building traditional networking equipment, one may assume a significant amount of networking knowledge. Imagine the impact of a new IoT standard on the number of network-ready manufacturers out there and the boost that would give to the worldwide economy.

Contrast this with the likely millions of firms and individuals worldwide building the kinds of simple sensors, actuators, and appliances which will be connected to the Internet of Things. It is inconceivable that all those makers of simple devices can be expected to queue up for addresses assigned by any centralized authority—or that rogue states, organizations, or individuals wouldn't attempt to subvert such systems.

Extending this thinking, simply scanning for hundreds of billions of IPv6 addresses would take literally hundreds of years. It is one thing to put addresses on nearly a trillion devices, but quite another to find and manage one device out of that constellation. The human cost to manage an Internet of Things made up solely of sophisticated IPv6 devices would exceed the cost of any networking project on earth to date. These costs will fall hardest on already strapped carriers that are already struggling to wring more revenue from expensive physical plant investments.

Only Where and When Needed

Of necessity, the emerging new architecture of the Internet of Things should take an entirely different approach, as described throughout this book. End devices have only locally meaningful and likely non-unique names. This is not a problem because there is networking intelligence elsewhere in the architecture at a much smaller (and thus more manageable) number of points.

And there is no need to oversee or control every maker of end devices. Because the IoT provides only limited networking capabilities at the end devices, there is little "harm" they can do on the network as a whole, and this is easily controlled through a much smaller number of "smarter" devices."

This approach is totally different from IPv6, which demands that every device have the functionality and management to act as a "peer" on the network. The Internet of Things simply cannot scale if built of peers that all must be managed. Like a massive ant colony, the IoT will scale through specialization, individual autonomy, and localized effect. In this way, costs are reduced by orders of magnitude.

Security Through Simplicity (and Stupidity)

A trite statement, but ultimately true. Because the communications with the end devices in this emerging architecture of the Internet of Things are so basic and so specialized, there are limited back doors and security risks. Again, contrast this with the "peer-to-peer" world of the IPv6 Internet where many IP devices are exposed to hacking and cracking attempts from anywhere in the world. The global cost of Internet security breaches has been estimated at $115 billion (Symantec, 2012). With roughly 2.4 billion peer-to-peer nodes on the Internet today, this roughly equates to $50 per node (user) per year in losses. Multiplying that figure times the projected hundreds of billions of Internet of Things devices creates an unsustainably high cost of IPv6 in the IoT.

By focusing on limited networking capabilities for the end devices as described in this book, the emerging architecture of the Internet of Things drastically reduces the risks and costs associated with networking the huge population of appliances, actuators, and sensors.

Cost and Connectivity

The key for the expected expansion of the Internet of Things is connecting hundreds of billions more devices at far-reduced costs and risks. Only this emerging IoT architecture can accomplish both in a way that is cost-effective for device manufacturers, Internet carriers, and users.

Solving the IoT Dilemma

With the economic and technology challenges posed by the number and unmanageable nature of the end devices of the Internet of Things well-defined, the next step is to investigate solutions. The balance of this chapter, and indeed this book, is devoted to exploring the concepts which may be used to create an architecture (working side by side with, and enhancing the potential of, the traditional IP network) for the Internet of Things that may practically scale to the size and scope required.

Inspiration for a New Architecture

So if traditional networking architectures are not appropriate for all the potential applications of the Internet of Things, where can solutions be found? In addressing this question, fields as diverse as robotics, embedded systems, big data, and wireless mesh networking contribute concepts and technology, although none of these directly addresses the scale and scope of the Internet of Things, nor the simplicity of the vast majority of IoT end points.

There are no human-produced technology systems that scale to the massive size of the imminent IoT. So when considering techniques and processes, it is necessary to turn to nature, in which systems have evolved that scale to hundreds of billions of individual elements exchanging information (broadly defined) in some fashion. It quickly becomes clear that the only highly optimized systems exhibiting this sort of scope are populations of the natural world: colonies of social insects, the propagation of pollen, the dissemination of larval young, and so on.

Nature: The Original Big Data

The most obvious similarity between the natural systems and the emerging Internet of Things is scale—natural systems are truly massive. Billions and billions of individuals operate and interact as a population (of one species) or an ecosystem (of many species). Visual, aural, and chemical signals are broadcast and interpreted; gametes such as pollen may be distributed over vast areas by wind and currents to interact with other individuals of the same species; and huge groups of similar and dissimilar organisms share information about threats or food sources (intentionally or incidentally).

Obviously, the communication of these natural systems is not centrally controlled, nor are there elaborate protocols or retransmission schemes in place. Instead, species have evolved within the natural world in ways that make this communication possible. What are these characteristics that make this "networking" possible in the massive systems of nature?

Autonomy of Individuals

One of the most striking things about natural systems is the way in which individuals independently send and receive communications and act on the information. Even seemingly highly organized populations or colonies such as ant and bee colonies are actually made up of individuals making decisions independently. Because individuals make these choices based on simple algorithms (usually dichotomous decision points) that are shared by all, the actions of the colony as a whole are as efficient as if centrally directed.

Even more remarkably, the actual brain "computing power" available to many species in nature is quite limited. Yet they can act on stimuli, communicate threats, broadcast mating availability, and perform many other tasks vital for survival. In the natural model, the simplicity of the individual is balanced by a narrowly defined purpose to its communications.

In the same way, most individual end devices in the IoT can be (indeed must be) very simple and autonomous. As noted previously, it will not be economically or architecturally feasible to burden these billions of devices with large amounts of computing power, memory, or protocol sophistication. When powered up, these devices must begin sending or receiving data immediately with no setup, management, or other interaction. It is interesting to note that many social insects operate in much the same way; immediately upon emerging in adult form, they begin a task such as nurturing nearby young. Without this autonomy of function and independence of individuals' actions, nature would not scale—and neither can the IoT.

Zones and Neighborhoods of Interest

Another aspect of natural systems that allow them to scale is the evolution of "zones" or "neighborhoods" of interest formed by "affinities," which allow individuals to act upon a specific signal among countless other signals. A bird song is an interesting example of this phenomenon. Walking through a field, one may be struck by the songs being sung by several different bird species simultaneously. These songs can have a variety of purposes, such as advertising mating availability and suitability or defining territories.

But each individual takes note only of songs from members of its own species (see Figure 1-6). The zones of interest, or neighborhoods of interest, of various bird species can overlap, and one communications medium (in this case audible frequencies transmitted through the air) is being used for all messages. But each individual bird acts only upon messages within its own group. Similarly, a viable architecture for the IoT must allow interested observers to define a neighborhood of interest (within the much larger Internet) and analyze or send data only from or to that neighborhood.

Figure 1-6. *Although many different species of birds may be singing in a field, only members of the same species listen*

In the Eyes of the Beholder

Another important aspect of scaling in the natural world is that many communications are receiver-oriented. This is in direct contrast with the sender-oriented nature of many traditional communications protocols, as described previously. Plant pollen represents an interesting example of this highly scalable characteristic of natural systems.

Many of us view pollen as a (literal) irritant during hay fever season. But pollen's actual role in nature is in plant reproduction. Pollen released by the male plant is carried indiscriminately by the wind. Because pollen is a lightweight (again, literally) signal, it can be distributed hundreds or even thousands of miles by air currents. At some point, pollen falls randomly out of the air, landing on any surface. The vast majority of released pollen falls on bodies of water, bare ground, streets, or plants of another species, where it deteriorates with no effect. But some tiny portion of the total pollen released falls upon the appropriate flowering parts of a female plant of the same species. At this point, pollination takes place and seeds are generated for the next generation (see Figure 1-7).

Figure 1-7. *In nature, only the "correct" receivers act on "messages" received, such as pollen. All others discard or ignore the message*

The communication of pollen is thus *receiver-oriented*. The zone or neighborhood of interest is defined by the receiving plant, which ignores all other signals (pollen from other species). The overall network (winds and so on) does not discriminate or actively manage the transmission of pollen in any way; it's merely a transport mechanism. The "intelligence" of nature is applied *only at the receiver*.

In the same way, a *scalable* architecture for the Internet of Things out of necessity includes many elements that are receiver-oriented, with zones or neighborhoods of interest being applied at the point of data integration and collection. These integrator functions will build interesting streams of data from "neighborhoods" that are geographical, temporal, or functional.

Another way of expressing these natural-world communications interactions is in term of publishers and subscribers. Many individuals may "publish" information in the form of calls, visual displays, pollen, etc. But these are moot unless other individuals "subscribe" to these messages. There is no set relationship between publisher and subscriber, as there would be in the peer-to-peer world of traditional networking–the natural world is simply too large and (obviously) unmanaged. In the IoT, the principle is the same: the only way to fully extract information from the myriad possible sources is through publish/subscribe relationships, which can scale.

Signal Simplicity

In the preceding examples from nature, most "signals" are simple and have a single purpose. This makes them "lightweight" and easily transported through the environment, even to the fringes or frontiers of a territory. With a single purpose, they are also easily "analyzed" and acted upon at their destination. (Contrast this with the general-purpose nature of traditional networking protocols, designed with overhead sufficient to support transport of a wide variety of payloads).

Similarly, the vast majority of data transported in the Internet of Things will be very simple and single-purposed in function. Many sensor-type end devices will be communicating only simple states or conditions. If they receive any data at all, it will be simple "sets" defining minor configuration changes. Other types of devices may send nothing and receive only simple instructions or settings from a central source or function.

Besides being lightweight, another key element of natural communications, such as the broadcast of pollen, is that the individual messages are *self-classified*. Pollen particles exhibit a particular size and shape that "key" them to specific receivers. Bacteria and viruses are likewise structured to interact with specific hosts. These natural messages are classified for type and content *externally*, that is, by their shape or form. Similarly, messages in the emerging IoT will have external markers that will allow action by intermediate network elements.

Leveraging Nature

Bringing all these concepts found in nature into the emerging architecture of the Internet of Things is inherently a more organic approach. The key lesson from nature is that huge scale is possible only with simple building blocks. Rather than building upon already bloated networking protocols, the architecture of the IoT must be based upon the minimum networking requirements—with only the minimal complexity added at the precise points at which it is needed.

Peer-to-Peer Is Not Equal

Because most Internet of Things communications will be machine-to-machine, it can be tempting to consider the IoT a peer-to-peer network: the general concept of peer-to-peer architectures is extremely attractive. The prospect of billions of devices seamlessly interacting with one another would seem to allow the Internet of Things to escape the limitations of centralized command and control, instead taking full advantage of Metcalf's Law to create more value through more interconnections.

But true peer-to-peer communication isn't perfect democracy; it's senseless cacophony. In the IoT, many devices at the edge of the network have no need to be connected with other devices at the edge of the network—there is zero value in the information (see Figure 1-8). As described previously, these devices have simple needs to speak and hear: perhaps sharing a few bytes of data *per hour* on bearing temperature and fuel supply for a diesel generator. Again, burdening them with protocol stacks, processing, and memory to allow true peer-to-peer networking is a complete waste of resources and creates more risk of failures, management and configuration errors, and hacking. More-sophisticated end devices may still require IP and they can exist side by side with simpler devices and be optimally served by technologies required to maximize the potential of the Internet of Things (as will be discussed in Chapter 7).

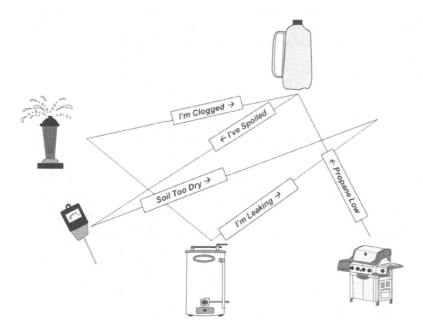

Figure 1-8. *Machine-to-machine interconnection between devices at the network edge are unnecessary: toaster-to-printer, for example*

Transporting IoT Traffic

There is obviously a need to transport the data destined to (or originating from) these edge devices. The desired breakthrough for a truly universal IoT is to use increasing degrees of intelligence and networking capability to manage that transportation of data at various points in the network—but not to burden *every* device with the *same* degree of networking capability.

Billions of Devices; Three Functional Levels

To this point, the economic and practical reasons for a new architecture for the Internet of Things have been described. In addition, lessons from massively scaling systems in nature have been explored as possible models for communications in the IoT, along with the arguments for keeping the burden of communications very low on the simple end devices that will form the vast majority of the Internet of Things.

But if the communications intelligence and functionality does not exist within the end devices, other devices to transport data efficiently must be found elsewhere in the network. And if the data being sent and received by end devices is to be of any use, there must be elements of the network outside of the end devices to manage that data flow.

The most powerful concept of the emerging architecture of the Internet of Things is division of the network into three functional classes, allowing deployment of networking functionality (and cost and complexity) only where and when needed. These three classes are:

- The end devices

- *Propagator nodes* providing transport and gateways to the traditional Internet

- *Integrator functions* offering analysis, control, and human interfaces to the IoT

At the edge of the network are the simple end devices, which are represented on the left in Figure 1-9. They transmit or receive their small amounts of data in a variety of ways: wirelessly over any number of protocols, via power line networking, or by being directly connected to a higher-level device. These edge devices simply "speak" their small amounts of data or listen for data directed toward them. (The means of handling this addressing will be discussed in detail in Chapter 6.)

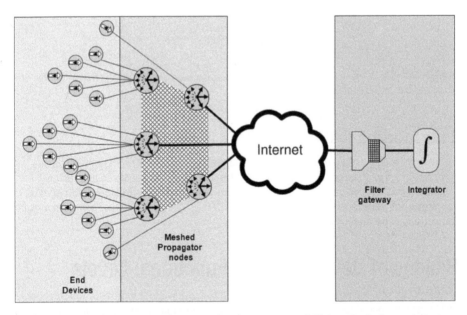

Figure 1-9. *The emerging architecture for the Internet of Things includes end devices, propagator nodes, and integrator functions*

Unlike traditional protocols such as IPv6, the IoT architecture involves no error-checking, routing, higher-level addressing, or anything of the sort at the end devices. That's because none of these is needed. Edge devices (Level I, so to speak) are fairly mindless "worker bees" existing on a minimum of data flow. This will suffice for the overwhelming majority of devices connected to the IoT.

Propagator Nodes Add Networking Functionality

The protocol intelligence resides elsewhere in the IoT network: within the Level II *propagator nodes shown in the mesh in Figure* 1-9. They are technologically a bit more like familiar traditional networking equipment such as routers, but they operate in a different way. Propagator nodes listen for data originating from any device. Based on a simple set of rules regarding the "arrow" of transmission (toward devices or away from devices), propagator nodes decide how to broadcast these transmissions to other propagator nodes or to the higher-level *integrator* devices discussed in the next section.

In order to scale to the immense size of the Internet of Things, these propagator nodes must be capable of a great deal of discovery and self-organization. They will recognize other propagator nodes within range, set up simple routing tables of adjacencies, and discover likely paths to the appropriate integrators. Similar challenges have been solved before with wireless mesh networking technology (among many others), and although the topology algorithms are complex, the amount of data exchange needed is small.

One of the important capabilities of propagator nodes is being able to prune and optimize broadcasts. Data passing from and to end devices may be combined with other traffic and forwarded in the general direction of their transmission "arrow." Propagator nodes are perhaps the closest functional elements to the traditional idea of peer-to-peer networking, but they provide networking on behalf of end devices and integrator functions at levels "above" and "below" themselves. Any of the standard networking protocols can be used, and propagator nodes will perform important translation functions between different networks (power line or Bluetooth to ZigBee or Wi-Fi, for example).

Although the preceding describes the generic function of the propagator nodes, many will also incorporate an important additional capability: the capacity to be managed and "tuned" by integrator functions across the network. This will take the form of a software *publishing agent* within fully featured propagator nodes. As more fully described in Chapters 4 and 5, this publishing agent will become part of the information "neighborhood" created by one or more integrator functions. In much the same manner as a Software Defined Network, the integrator function will apply higher-level management to particular propagator nodes, controlling functions such as frequency of data transmission, network topology, and other networking functionality.

Collecting, Integrating, Acting

Integrator functions are where the data streams from hundreds to millions of devices are analyzed and acted upon. Integrator functions also send their own transmissions to get information or set values at devices—of course, the transmission arrow of this data is pointed toward devices. Integrator functions may also incorporate a variety of inputs, from big data to social networking trends, and from Facebook "likes" to weather reports.

In this emerging architecture, integrator functions are the *human* interface to the IoT. As such, they will be built to reduce the unfathomably large amounts of data collected over a period of time to a simple set of alarms, exceptions, and other reports for consumption by humans. In the other direction, they will be used to manage the IoT by biasing devices to operate within certain desired parameters.

Using simple concepts such as "cluster" and "avoid" (discussed in Chapter 5), integrated scheduling and decision-making processes within the integrator functions allow much of the IoT to operate transparently and *without human intervention.* One integrator function might be needed for an average household operating on a smartphone, computer, or home entertainment device. Or the integrator function could be scaled up to a huge global enterprise, tracking and managing energy usage across a corporation, for example. (Integrator functions are fully explored in Chapter 5.)

When the Scope Is Too Massive

An additional device at this third level of the architecture is the *filter gateway.* Filter gateways are notionally two-armed routers, with a connection to the Internet and a connection to the integrator function. Integrator functions are general purpose processors like PCs and can be overwhelmed by very large amounts of data, denial-of-service attacks, and so on. So the filter gateway is an appliance that ensures that only meaningful data is forwarded to the integrator function. Filter gateways may use a simple set of rules (set by the attached integrator function) to filter the traffic presented to the integrator, restricting it to the "neighborhood of interest" only. These neighborhoods again can be geographic, functional, time-based, or some combination of many other factors.

Functional vs. Physical Packaging

When it comes to actually packaging and delivering products, some physical devices will certainly be combinations of architectural elements. Propagator nodes combined with one or more end devices certainly make sense, as will other combinations (see Figure 1-10). But the important concept here is to replace the idea of peer-to-peer for everything with a *graduated* amount of networking delivered *as needed* and *where needed.* In the Internet of Things, a division of labor is required (such as in ant and bee colonies) so that devices with not much to say or hear receive only the amount of networking they need–and no more.

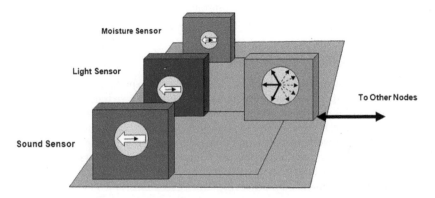

Figure 1-10. Some devices incorporate multiple IoT functions in a single package. Here multiple end devices are combined with a propagator node that may provide networking services for additional nearby end devices

Connecting to the "Big I"

To this point, this chapter has focused on the characteristics and functions that differentiate the Internet of Things from the traditional Internet (or "Big I").

Despite the clear and compelling reasons for a new architecture and protocol at the very *edge* of the Internet of Things, it is not possible to escape a fundamental truth: in order to scale to billions of devices worldwide, the traditional Internet is the *only viable* backbone for transporting IoT traffic. So at some point, the lightweight IoT protocols must be packaged or converted to traditional Internet protocols that may take advantage of the deployed worldwide Internet architecture.

As briefly noted previously and more fully explored in Chapter 6, the architecture of the Internet of Things provides trunking and conversion functionality at richly featured propagator nodes. Less-featured propagator nodes also exist that communicate only with lightweight IoT protocols, depending on other propagator nodes for IP conversion. This is described in detail in Chapter 4.

Thus, connections between propagator nodes may be either traditional protocols such as IPv6 or lightweight IoT protocols. More importantly, richly featured propagator nodes will provide conversion to IPv6 for routing data between end devices and their associated integrator functions. In turn, integrator functions also typically include IPv6 for direct Internet connectivity (or it can be provided by a filter gateway).

Smaller Numbers, Bigger Functionality

In addition, there is a relatively small number (still billions) of more-sophisticated end devices connected to the Internet of Things that incorporate mission-critical data, greater data requirements, and/or real–time data needs. These devices can justify the costs and complexity of processing, memory, and a full protocol stack, so they will connect directly via IPv6. An example is a video surveillance camera or complex process controller.

IPv6 data to and from these devices may still be combined with lightweight IoT data streams at the same integrator functions. In addition, interesting hybrid devices can develop that include both a lightweight IoT interface *and* a traditional IPv6 connection. In these situations, the lightweight IoT protocols might be used for normal or routine communications, with the IPv6 connections becoming active based on a particular event or condition.

Fundamentally, the IoT network protocols must coexist and interoperate with the traditional Internet and other networks such as Cellular 4G and LTE. The key challenge for the emerging Internet of Things architecture is to allow this interoperability without burdening the billions and billions of simpler end devices. The next chapter describes the simple "chirp" structure of IoT data and how it is delivered across the Internet of Things.

CHAPTER 2

■ ■ ■

Anatomy of the Internet of Things

It may appear to be a daunting task to engineer a new networking architecture for the Internet of Things (IoT). Yet nothing less than a completely new approach is needed. The Internet of Things environment is so different, and the devices to be connected so varied, that there has never been a networking challenge quite like it since the origin of what is now called the Internet.

In developing this new architecture for the Internet of Things, key lessons have been drawn from the development of the traditional Internet and other transformational technologies to provide some basic guiding principles:

- It should specify as little as possible and leave much open for others to innovate.

- Systems must be designed to fail gracefully: seeking not to eliminate errors, but to accommodate them.

- Graduated degrees of networking functionality and complexity are applied only where and when needed.

- The architecture is created from simple concepts that build into complex systems using the analog provided by natural phenomena.

- Meaning may be extracted from data in real time.

The emerging architecture for the Internet of Things is intended to be more inclusive of a wider variety of market participants by reducing the amount of networking knowledge and resources needed at the edges of the network. This architecture must also be extremely tolerant of failures, errors, and intermittent connections at this level. (Counter intuitively, the best approach is to *simplify* protocols at the edge rather than to make them more complex.)

In turn, increasing sophistication of networking capabilities are applied at gateways into the traditional Internet, in which propagator nodes provide communications services for armies of relatively unsophisticated devices.

Finally, meaning can be extracted from the universe of data in integrator functions that provide the human interface to the Internet of Things. This level of oversight is applied only at the highest level of the network; simpler devices, like worker bees in a hive, need not be burdened with computational or networking resources.

To explore what's needed for this new architecture, it is first necessary to *abandon* the networking status quo.

Traditional Internet Protocols Aren't the Solution for Much of the IoT

When contemplating how the Internet of Things will work, it helps to *forget* the conventional wisdom regarding traditional networking schemes—especially wide area networking (WAN) and wireless networking. In traditional WAN and wireless networking, the bandwidth or spectrum is expensive and limited, and the amount of data to be transmitted is large and always growing. Although over-provisioning data paths in wiring the desktop (and a majority of the traditional Internet) is commonplace, this isn't usually practical in the WAN or wireless network—it's just too expensive. With carriers largely bearing the cost and passing it along to customers, wireless costs range as high as ten times the wired equivalents using IP.

Besides cost, there's the matter of potential data loss and (in the wireless world) collisions. Traditional networking protocols include lots of checks and double-checks on message integrity to minimize costly retransmissions. These constraints led to today's familiar protocol stacks, such as TCP/IP and 802.11.

Introducing the "Chirp"

In most of the Internet of Things, however, the situation is completely different. The costs of wireless and wide-area bandwidth are still high, to be sure. And because many of the connections at the edge of the network—the IoT frontier, so to speak—will be wireless and/or lossy, any Internet of Things architecture must address these factors. But the amounts of data from most devices will be almost *immeasurably low* and the delivery of any single message *completely uncritical*. As discussed previously, the IoT is lossy and intermittent, so the end devices will be designed to function perfectly well even if they miss sending or receiving data for a while—even for a long while. As discussed earlier, it is this self-sufficiency that eliminates the criticality of any *single* message.

After reviewing all existing options in considering the needs of the IoT architecture from the ground up, it is clearly necessary to define a new type of data frame or packet. This new type of packet offers only the amount of overhead and functionality needed for simple IoT devices at the edge of the network—*and no more*. These small data packets, which are called *chirps,* are the fundamental building block of the emerging architecture for the IoT. Chirps are different from traditional Internet protocol packets in many ways (see the "Why Not the IP for the IoT?" sidebar. Fundamental characteristics of chirps include the following:

- Chirps incorporate only minimal overhead payloads, "arrows" of transmission (see below), simple *non-unique* addresses, and modest checksums.

- Chirps are inherently individually noncritical by design.

- Therefore, chirps include no retransmission or acknowledgment protocols.

Any additional functions necessary for carrying chirp traffic over the traditional Internet, such as global addressing, routing, and so on, are handled autonomously by other network devices by means of adding information to received simple chirps. There are therefore no provisions made for these functions within a chirp packet.

Lightweight and Disposable

In contrast to traditional networking packet structures, IoT chirps are like pollen or bird songs: lightweight, broadly propagated, and with meaning only to the "interested" integrator functions or end devices. The IoT is receiver-centric, not sender-centric, as is IP. Because IoT chirps are so small and *no individual chirp is critical*, there is limited concern over retries and resulting broadcast storms, which are a danger in IP.

It's true that efficient IoT propagator nodes will prune and bundle broadcasts (see Figure 2-1 and Chapter 4), but seasonal or episodic broadcast storms from end devices are much less of a problem because the chirps are small (and thus cause less congestion) and individually uncritical. Excessive chirps may thus be discarded by propagator nodes as necessary.

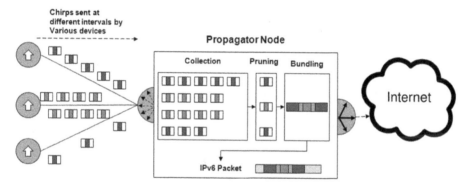

Figure 2-1. *Chirps are typically collected within propagator nodes, bundled and pruned as necessary for transmission, and then typically forwarded via IPv6 over the traditional Internet*

Functionality the IoT Needs—and Doesn't

This very different view of networking means that huge packets, security at the publisher, and assured delivery of any *single* message are unnecessary, allowing for massive networks based on extremely lightweight components. In one sense, this makes the IoT more "female" (receiver-oriented) than the "male" structure of IP (sender-oriented).

But there is obviously no point in having an IoT if nothing *ever* gets through. How can the acknowledged unpredictable nature of connections be managed? The answer, perhaps surprisingly, is over-provisioning—but only very locally between chirp device and propagator node. That is, these short, simple chirps may be re-sent over and over again as a brute-force means of ensuring that some get through.

Efficiency Out of Redundancy

As seen in Figure 2-2, because the chunks of data are so small, the costs of this over-provisioning at the very edge of the IoT are infinitesimal. (They are often handled by local Wi-Fi, Bluetooth, infrared, and so on, so they are not metered by any carrier.) Therefore, the benefits of this sort of scheme are huge. Because no individual message is critical, there's no need for any error-recovery or integrity-checking overhead (except for the most basic checksum to avoid a garbled message). Each chirp message simply has an address, a short data field, and a checksum. In some ways, these messages are what IP datagrams were meant to be. Chirps are also similar in many ways to the concepts of the Simple Network Management Protocol (SNMP), with simple "get" and "set" functionality.

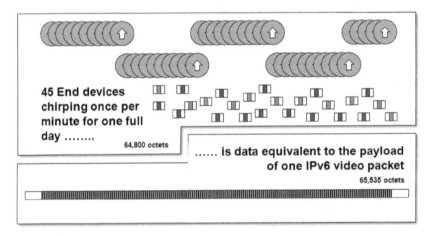

45 End devices chirping once per minute for one full day ....
64,800 octets

...... is data equivalent to the payload of one IPv6 video packet
65,535 octets

Figure 2-2. *Many small chirps (machine-to-machine–oriented) are still considerably less data than a much longer IP packet (human-oriented)*

Importantly, the cost and complexity burden on the end devices to incorporate chirp messaging will be very low–because it must be in the IoT. The most efficient integration schemes will likely be "chirp on a chip" approaches, with minimal data input/output and transmission/reception functionality combined in a simple standardized package.

The chirp will also incorporate the "arrow" of transmission mentioned previously, identifying the general direction of the message: whether toward end devices or toward integrator functions (see Figure 2-3). Messages moving to or from end devices need only the address of the end device; where it is headed or where it is from is *unimportant* to the vast majority of simple end devices. These devices are merely broadcasting and/or listening, and local relevancy or irrelevancy is all that matters.

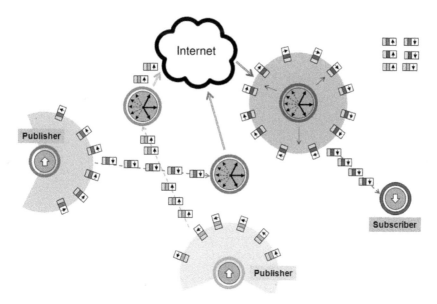

Figure 2-3. *Each chirp includes an "arrow" of transmission that indicates its direction of propagation: toward end devices or toward integrator functions*

So the end devices may be awash in the ebb and flow of countless transmissions. They may broadcast continuously and trust that propagator nodes and integrator functions elsewhere in the network will delete or ignore redundant messages. Likewise, they may receive countless identical messages before detecting one that has changed and requires an action in response.

In essence, this means that the chirp protocol is "wasteful" in terms of retransmissions only very locally, where bandwidth is cheap or free (essentially "off the net"). But because propagator nodes are designed to minimize the amount of superfluous or repeated traffic that is forwarded, WAN costs and traffic to the traditional Internet are vastly reduced.

Note that, unlike traditional network end devices such as smartphones and laptops, the largest percentage of IoT end devices likely *will not* include both send and receive functions (see Figure 2-4). An air quality sensor, for example, needs to send only the current state for whatever chemicals it is measuring. It begins sending when powered on, and repeatedly chirps this information until switched off. This may simplify significantly the hardware and embedded software needed at the vast majority of end points.

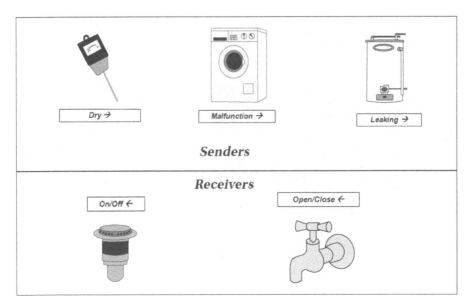

Figure 2-4. *Many IoT devices will be send-only or receive-only*

WHY NOT IP FOR THE IOT?

Although IPv6 already exists (and will at some point be ubiquitous within the traditional Internet), it is not the ideal format for much of the IoT traffic—for a variety of reasons outlined in Chapter 1 related to processing power and device memory that would be required in the tremendous quantity of otherwise simple and cheap end devices in the Internet of Things. But there are also fundamental protocol inefficiencies that make IPv6 unsuitable for the IoT, as discussed here. Still, there will be a vast array of end devices that must use IP, so a dual approach to protocols, IP, and the chirp protocols used together to service IoT devices of all kinds would yield an optimal result. It is worthwhile to compare and contrast the traditional IPv6 packet format with the IoT chirp, considering the difference in applications for which each is designed.

IP protocols were originally designed (in the early 1970s) for peer-to-peer communications between large hosts. These exchanges tended to be in large blocks of data, so IP is fundamentally oriented toward larger payloads. In addition, because WAN connections were extremely expensive and unreliable at the time when these host-to-host links were first designed, it was critical to incorporate the addresses of sender and receiver, as well as error detection and retransmission capabilities within the protocol to make it more robust. The result is that the header overhead of a single IPv6 packet is fairly high: 40 bytes. (A significant amount of the overhead in IP is dedicated to security, encryption, and other services, none of which matters at the very edges of the Internet of Things where the simplest devices predominate.)

Although originally imagined for machine-to-machine traffic, much of the IP traffic on the traditional Internet today is oriented toward human communications. This often consists of relatively long-duration sessions and some degree of full-duplex interaction over relatively costly links (at least until recently). Traditional networking protocols are thus designed for reliability and recoverability because nearly every packet is necessary for human context and understanding.

As a general-purpose protocol designed to carry data of virtually any type or degree of criticality, IP imposes at least this much overhead on every transmission. The structure of the header is strictly defined, and most aspects are unchangeable—the standard is absolute.

IP establishes Maximum Transmission Units (MTUs) that describe the maximum size of data blocks that the link is expected to carry. They have increased over time to 1,280 bytes for IPv6, although most deployed networks have MTUs of 1,500 or more. Peer-to-peer host traffic will tend to be managed by the applications to come in larger blocks to match outbound blocks to the MTU to maximize efficiency.

With packets of these sizes, the IP overhead is a relatively small percentage of the overall "cost" of transmission. For example, 40 bytes of IPv6 overhead added to a 1280 byte MTU is roughly 97% efficiency. In actual practice, the overhead is often doubled because an acknowledgment packet is required to be sent for each arriving packet. With no data payload, this acknowledgment packet is also the IPv6 minimum of 40 bytes. (In the host-to-host environment for which IP was originally designed, there would usually be some data to be sent in the return direction, though, so the overhead is not always wasted.)

But the Internet of Things is definitely not made up of peer-to-peer communications between like hosts. Because Internet of Things chirp traffic is machine-to-machine-oriented, it is by contrast sporadic, (nearly always) simplex, and almost free because of low volumes of data and low duty cycles. The IoT is a publish/subscribe model with very simple end devices transmitting or receiving only tiny amounts of individually noncritical pieces of data at one time. A temperature sensor output might be expressed in 8 bits or fewer, for example. So for a large number of similar applications, the data "payload" would be only 1 byte. Applying IPv6 to this application with the same overhead calculation yields 40 bytes of IPv6 overhead to 1 byte sensor data is only about 2% efficiency!

Chirps are designed to minimize overhead for this type of data in the multiple ways described in this chapter, such as simplifying addresses, eliminating retransmission overhead, and so on. Most importantly, the relative structure of the chip packet adds differing amounts of overhead depending on the type and size of the data generated by the end device, ensuring maximum efficiency. Only the smallest (4.5 byte total, 3.5 byte overhead) chirp packet would be needed to send an 8-bit payload, for an efficiency gain of roughly an order of magnitude over IPv6 (18% vs. 2%). See the comparison in Figure 2-5.

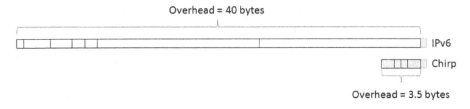

Comparison: Total packet length with 1 Byte Payload

Figure 2-5. *Comparison of TCP/IP packet and chirp packet overheads for a 1-byte payload from a simple sensor*

In general, larger data payloads result in more efficient chirp packets, with the headers increasing only incrementally to match specific applications, as further described in Chapter 6. For example, a 4-byte end-device payload could be handled with the same 3.5-byte overhead, for an efficiency of more than 50%.

One other critical differences between chirps and IP packets is that chirps are self-classified through external markers (see "Family Types" below). This makes it easy for integrator functions to discover new interesting data flows by looking for affinities with "known" data sources. The only way this could be accomplished in IP would be to include the classification information within the payload, which would require impractical deep inspection of every packet by propagator nodes and integrator functions.

So chirps make eminent sense in the "last mile" of network connections at the edge of the IoT frontier instead of IPv6. Beyond the edges of the network, the situation changes, however. Propagator-to-propagator or propagator-to-integrator communications can much more resemble host-to-host traffic because their transmissions may consist of bundled chirps to and from many end devices (increasing the size of the data blocks to be exchanged). In those situations, the error correction and other features of a protocol such as IP are more useful, as more fully described in Chapter 4. And because these communications often use the traditional Internet as the medium, it makes even more sense to simply use existing IPv6 networking protocol stacks.

Note that some sensitive and proprietary applications (government, security, financial, and so on) will remain that also require the additional features of IP in terms of guaranteed delivery, security, and so on. These types of applications are not part of the emerging Internet of Things as defined in this book and will, of course, remain on traditional protocols.

It's All Relative

The detailed structure of the chirp packet is described in Chapter 6, but a brief introduction is useful here. The key difference between the Internet of Things packet and other packet formats is that the meanings of values within the packet are _relative. That is, there is no fixed definition for the packet locating headers, addresses, and so on (as there is for IPv6, for example).

As seen in Figure 2-6, _markers_ are used in place of a fixed format definition to allow receiving devices to determine information such as sending address, type of sensor and data, arrow of transmission, and so on. These markers are both _public_ and _private_ types.

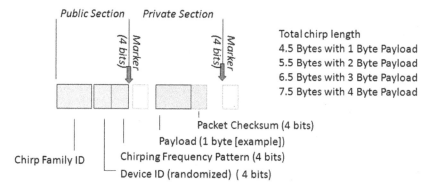

Figure 2-6. *The IoT chirp packet is unique in that addressing and other information is determined by relative position to defined markers, not by a rigid general overall protocol formats*

Public markers, which are found in every IoT packet, allow the receiving device to "parse" the incoming traffic. When a public marker is noted, the receiving device examines data ahead of and behind the marker for specific bits needed to determine how the rest of the packet will be forwarded and/or acted upon. The receiving device need not examine the packet except for the areas indicated by the location and type of public marker observed. Public markers include the basic arrow of transmission described previously, a limited 4-bit checksum for packet verification, and so on. Bits in the data field that are not part of the routing and verification information are simply treated as a data payload at this level of examination.

Format Flexibility

The presence of public markers within the IoT chirp packet permits the length of the IoT packet to vary as necessary for the specific application, device type, or message format. Different families of IoT packets with varying amounts of public data fields are defined to allow sufficient information to be added for applications that need additional context, but also to allow for minimal overhead for the most basic device types and generic IoT packet propagation.

The use of public markers is inspired by nature, including the transcription or "reading" of heredity information coded in DNA within genes to create proteins needed for development and life. DNA strands may contain repetitions and "junk" sections that should not be read, but localized markers are used to indicate "start" and "stop" points for transcription. Receiving devices use public markers in the same way to examine IoT chirp packets without requiring specific byte counts or other overhead-generating restrictions.

Private Markers for Customization and Extensibility

Private markers are permitted within the generic "data" field defined by public markers to allow customization of data formats for specific applications, manufacturers, and so on. As with public markers, the private marker allows a receiving device to parse the data stream to locate information for specific needs.

Addressing and "Rhythms"

As noted earlier, billions of end devices of the IoT will be extremely inexpensive and may be manufactured by makers throughout the world, many of whom will not have extensive networking knowledge. For this reason, ensuring address uniqueness through a centralized database of device addresses for the hundreds of billions of IoT end points is a nonstarter.

Part of the public information in the IoT chirp packet will be a simple, non-unique, 4-bit device ID applied through PC board traces, hardware straps, DIP switches, or similar means. As described in Chapter 6, it will combine with a randomly generated 4-bit pattern to ensure a much lower potential for two end devices, connected to the same local propagator node, to have identical identifications. (This combination of bits is also used to vary transmission rates in wireless environments to avoid a "deadly embrace.")

If additional addressing specificity and/or security is required in particular applications, it will be possible to add this information within the private space of the IoT packet.

Family Types

The final public information contained in all IoT chirp packets is a classification into one of 255 possible chirp "families." As described in Chapter 6, these families will primarily divide along type and application lines, such as sensors of various types, control valves, green/yellow/red status indicators, and so on. These chirp families will be defined from generic to more specific, and will be broad and extensible enough to allow any type of IoT application. As noted previously, for specific applications or devices in which more granularity of type classification is desired, this custom information may be defined by private markers within the data field.

The type and classification of the chirp packets enables one of the most far-reaching benefits of the IoT: the ability for data analyzers to discover and recruit new data sources based on affinities with information neighborhoods. Because this type and classification information is "external", it may be recognized and acted upon by many IoT elements, such as integrator functions and propagator nodes (along with their associated publishing agents, if so-equipped).

In this way, integrator functions monitoring a pressure sensor in a pipeline might seek out nearby temperature sensors to look for correlations that might provide richer information. The type and classification of the chirp packet alone conveys some potential knowledge that may be analyzed and coordinated with other information, and this is carried throughout the network as chirp packet streams are forwarded.

This feature is true even if the transmitting sensors were installed for a different application, by a different organization, or at a different point in time. The option for "public" advertising of type and classification allow broader use (and re-use) of chirp streams, by enabling dynamic publish/subscribe relationships to be created and modified over time as the IoT "learns".

This benefit is achieved without burdening end devices. Because most end devices are by definition very simple in the Internet of Things, those designed to receive IoT chirp packets will be required to process only the most basic of elements of the protocol (for example, using public markers to identify packets addressed to themselves and reading only that data). The IoT elements making much more extensive use of the capabilities of the chirp packet are those that must route or analyze data from many end devices, specifically the propagator nodes and integrator functions. These are the propagator nodes and integrator functions, described briefly next and in more detail in Chapters 4 and 5.

Applying Network Intelligence at Propagator Nodes

As noted previously, replicating even this highly efficient chirp protocol traffic indiscriminately throughout the IoT would clearly choke the network, so intelligence must be applied at levels above the individual end devices. This is the responsibility of *propagator nodes*, which are devices that create an overarching network topology to organize the sea of machine-to-machine interactions that make up the Internet of Things.

Propagator nodes are typically a combination of hardware and software distantly similar to WiFi access points. They handle "local" end devices, meaning that they interact with end devices essentially within the (usually) wireless transmission range of the propagator node. They can be specialized or used to receive chirps from a wide array of end devices. Eventually, there would be tens or perhaps hundreds of thousands of propagator nodes in a city like Las Vegas. Propagator nodes will use their knowledge of adjacencies to form a near-range picture of the network. They will locate in-range nearby propagator nodes, as well as end devices and integrator functions either attached directly to or reached via those propagator nodes. This information is used to create the network topology: eliminating loops and creating alternate paths for survivability.

The propagator nodes will intelligently package and prune the various chirp messages before broadcasting them to adjacent nodes. Examining the public markers, the simple checksum, and the "arrow" of transmission (toward end devices or toward integrator functions), damaged or redundant messages will be discarded. Groups of messages that are all to be propagated via an adjacent node may be bundled into one "meta" message-a small data "stream"-for efficient transmission. Arriving "meta" messages may be unpacked and repacked.

Some classes of propagator nodes will contain a software publishing agent (see Chapter 4). This publishing agent interacts with particular integrator functions to optimize data forwarding on behalf of the integrator. Propagator nodes with publishing agents may be "biased" to forward certain information in particular directions based on routing instructions passed down from the integrator functions interested in communicating with a particular functional, temporal, or geographic "neighborhood" of end devices. (Neighborhoods formed by integrator functions are further described in Chapter 5.) It is the integrator functions that will dictate the overall communications flow based on their needs to get data or set parameters in a neighborhood of IoT end devices.

In terms of discovery of new end devices, propagator nodes and integrator functions will be again similar to traditional networking architectures. When messages from or to new end devices appear, propagator nodes will forward them and add the addresses to their tables (see Figure 2-7). Appropriate age-out algorithms will allow for pruning the tables of adjacencies for devices that go offline or are mobile and are only passing through.

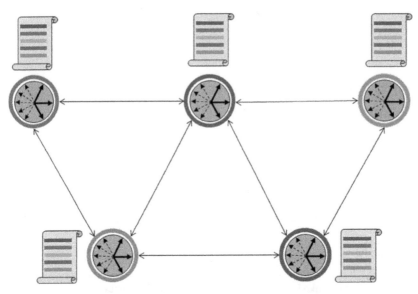

Figure 2-7. *Propagator nodes independently build routing tables (and thus, the network topology) based on the discovery of adjacent propagator nodes. Although not shown here, the location of integrator functions and discovered end devices would also be included in the makeup of the topology*

Transport and Functional Architectures

The emerging architecture of the Internet of Things combines two completely independent network topologies or architectures: *transport* and *functional*, as shown in Figure 2-8. The transport architecture is the infrastructure over which all traffic is moved and is provided primarily by propagator nodes (and the global Internet). The functional architecture is the virtual "zone" or "neighborhood" of interest created by integrator functions independent of physical paths.

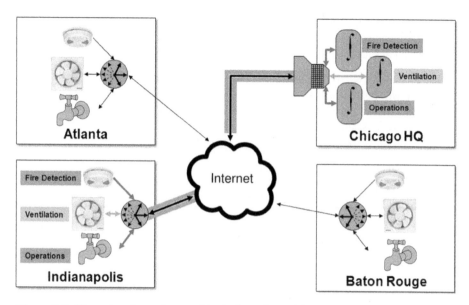

Figure 2-8. *The network topology and logical topology of the Internet of Things can vary considerably*

The transport network portion of the Internet of Things operates with little or no context of the actual significance of the data chirps being handled. As noted previously, propagator nodes build the transport network based on more-traditional networking concepts and routing algorithms (see Chapter 4). End chirp devices may link to propagator nodes in a wide variety of ways: wirelessly via radio or optical wavelengths (see the following "Chirps in a Wireless World" sidebar), power line networking, a direct physical connection, and so on. A single propagator node can be connected to a large number of chirp devices and provide services for all. Unless the propagator node is biased by the integrator function, the basic model is "promiscuous forwarding."

CHIRPS IN A WIRELESS WORLD

One other aspect of communication to be addressed within the Internet of Things is the matter of wireless networking. It's likely that many of the end device chirp connections in the IoT will be wireless, using a wide variety of frequencies and formats. This fact seems to suggest a need for something such as Carrier Sense Multiple Access with Detection (CSMA/CD), as used in 802.11 WiFi. But that's another aspect of traditional networking that must be forgotten.

Again, data rates will be very small, and most individual transmissions are completely uncritical. Even in a location with many devices vying for airtime, the overall duty cycle will be very low. And most messages will be duplicates, from our earlier principle of over-provisioning at the edge through repetition. With that in mind, an occasional collision is of zero significance. All that must be avoided is a "deadly embrace," in which multiple devices, unaware of one another's presence, continue transmitting at exactly the same time and colliding over and over.

The solution is a simple randomization of transmission times at every device, perhaps with continuously varying pauses between transmissions based on prime numbers, hashed end device address, or some other factors that provide uniquely varying transmission events.

Although the resulting communication scheme is very different from traditional networking protocols, it is all that is necessary for the IoT. Providing just enough communication at very low cost and complexity is a general IoT architectural principle and will be "good enough" for the Internet of Things.

As will be discussed in Chapter 4, propagator nodes bundle and convert chirp traffic as necessary for transport to adjacent propagator nodes and thence to integrator functions or chirp devices. The link between propagator nodes is typically a traditional networking protocol such as TCP/IP, but it can also be chirp-based.

Besides transporting the very simple chirps, the higher-level protocol packets created by the propagator nodes include additional contextual information not found in the chirps. This data may include additional address information related to location, time of day, and other factors, as shown in Figure 2-9. Thus, the propagator nodes increase the utility of the chirp data stream without burdening the vast numbers of end devices with networking cost and complexity. This additional contextual information is added only by propagator nodes and analyzed by integrator functions.

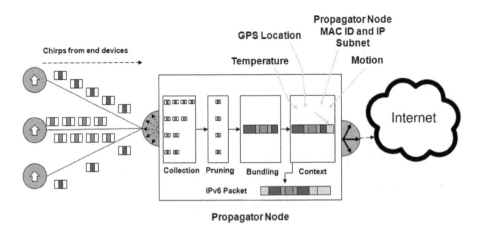

Figure 2-9. *As chirps are bundled within propagator nodes, additional location, addressing, protocol, and other information is added*

An important difference between the IoT transport architecture and many forms of traditional networking is that it is fundamentally egalitarian, similar to wind currents carrying all types of plant pollen. Propagator nodes will forward IoT traffic to and from *any* end device or integrator function within the constraints of "trust," "communications," and "control" factors (these will be outlined in Chapter 6). The IoT can then "piggyback" on existing infrastructure, and each new propagator node may increase functionality for a variety of users and integrator functions. Fundamentally, the transport network topology and architecture does not create (or limit) the *functional* IoT network topology, which is created by integrator functions.

Functional Network Topology

With the transport network architecture (described previously) providing forwarding services for chirps in both directions ("down" toward chirp devices and "up" toward integrator functions), attention may now be turned to the functional IoT architecture, which is overlaid on the transport architecture in somewhat the same way that the propagation of pollen is overlaid on general wind currents in the atmosphere.

The functional network of the IoT, then, becomes less a matter of how the "wires" (physical or virtual) are connected and much more a matter of information that is of interest. The emerging architecture of the Internet is fundamentally a "publish and subscribe" model driven by the integrator functions. It is also receiver-oriented, with the machine at the far end of the transmission "arrow" determining what data is pertinent and useful.

Defined by Integrator Functions

At this point, a brief description of the integrator function is appropriate, with more detail found in Chapter 5. Integrator functions may take a wide array of physical forms, and multiple logical integrator functions can be deployed on one machine with a single connection to the traditional Internet (perhaps via a filter gateway). From a functional standpoint, they are somewhat autonomous creators of relationships with a select group of end points.

As an example, imagine an integrator function designed to monitor moisture content in the far-flung fields of an agribusiness concern (see Figure 2-10). The moisture–sensing end devices broadcast chirps at intervals, indicating the moisture content of the surrounding soil. The tiny chirps of data have a transport "arrow" pointing toward integrator functions.

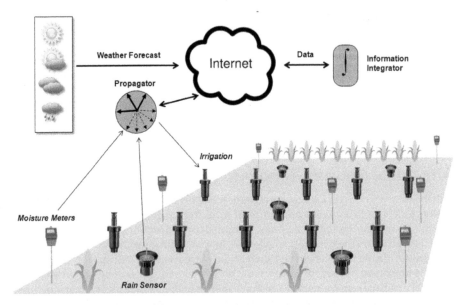

Figure 2-10. *An integrator function retrieves data from end devices such as moisture sensors and external feeds such as the expected precipitation and humidity, using the information to control irrigation valves*

The chirps are received by in-range propagator nodes deployed by the agribusiness concern (or anyone else). As noted previously, these chirps leave the propagator nodes bundled with additional contextual information such as a full IPv6 address and location information, allowing a more precise location and identification of the specific individual sensor that is not available from the simple chirp. The transport network of the propagator node essentially "publishes" these data streams via the traditional Internet.

Harvesting Information from the IoT

The preceding description suggests a virtual private sensor network, with a single agribusiness supplier installing its own end-device sensor propagator nodes, using the traditional Internet to create a routing path, and then monitoring the network privately for its own benefit. And certainly many IoT big data "neighborhoods" are created in this way. But there is also a tremendous potential for building networks that rely on data provided by Internet of Things elements not owned, managed, and controlled by a single source.

In the emerging social networking culture in the Western world, crowd sourcing and data sharing is becoming more commonplace. In light of this, individuals and organizations may choose to install sensors, cameras, and other devices of all kinds locally, providing the IoT streams from these devices generically and publicly. (Note that many individuals and groups do this today with web cams, weather sensors, and the like using traditional Internet protocols such as IP).

Propagator nodes set to promiscuously forward generic chirps would simply move these packets in the general direction of integrator functions. (Note that it is possible for propagator nodes to be used for both private and public streams simultaneously—offering transport for the general good, as it were.)

An integrator function might be configured, then, to gather data from interesting end devices that it has discovered by searching out small data streams from specific classes of device, location, or other characteristics. These integrator functions might combine small data streams from many independent end devices installed by any number of unknown individuals to create interesting new big data information.

Programming and "Bias"

Human programming of the integrator function may instruct it to look for certain locations and types of data streams via the traditional Internet, or the integrator functions may identify potentially interesting candidate data streams through affinities with known sources. Locating appropriate moisture sensor streams on the Internet, the integrator function begins to receive and incorporate this data. The integrator function may even "bias" the publishing agent within propagator nodes (if so-equipped) for some efficiency in combining chirps into larger packets in small data streams or discarding duplicate chirps. (Attached filter gateways might also serve to prune and select from verbose streams in the same way. This topic is more fully discussed in Chapter 5).

The human programming of the integrator function may now incorporate these streams of data on moisture content to look for changes that represent drying out beyond preset thresholds. Additional data, such as weather reports, air temperature, and irrigation reservoir levels (acquired from a variety of sources and feeds, both chirp-based and via the traditional Internet), might also be incorporated to provide a complete picture of irrigation needs for current and future periods of time.

The resulting reports might be provided for human action. Or, in a more automated scenario, the integrator function might respond (via its programming) to change watering times or durations in specific fields (if irrigation valves are also under IoT control). In this application, the integrator function might also analyze video surveillance streams to confirm that sprinklers are on and operating normally.

Note that this functional IoT network might interconnect over any transport topology. The agribusiness need not build out its own private network for the entire transport path; instead, it can use the traditional Internet for much of the transport infrastructure. The enterprise might deploy only the moisture sensors and some specialized propagator nodes, as appropriate.

This is only one example out of millions that might be imagined for the Internet of Things. But the basic principles of very simple devices at the edge, publish-and-subscribe, utilization of public network transport, and integration of a variety of data sources apply broadly.

Receiver-Oriented Selectivity

In the same way that female plants "select" only the appropriate pollen from the same species and reject foreign pollen, dust, and other material, integrator functions are similarly selective in choosing which chirp streams to incorporate as inputs for analysis.

Integrator functions may be programmed to "set," configure, or otherwise manipulate end devices by generating "chirp" traffic of their own that is packaged for routing through the traditional Internet to a propagator known to be near the target end device. With the transmission "arrow" set in the direction of end devices, these packets are transported to the appropriate propagator node (typically within IPv6 packets) and then output as IoT chirps. Integrator functions may combine chirps for widely scattered end devices in a single broadcast packet, which is then pruned and rebroadcast as necessary by intermediate propagator nodes.

The end devices may be able to "hear" a variety of traffic, but thanks to similar receiver-oriented selectivity, they act upon only the specific traffic intended for them. As noted earlier, the intermediate routing and addressing information is primarily a function of the propagator nodes; end devices need only detect the simple IoT chirp addresses.

The following chapter will detail the IoT architecture relating to end devices and will include suggested implementation strategies and alternatives.

CHAPTER 3

■ ■ ■

On the Edge

Although the backbone architectures of networks garner the most attention, the *actual drivers* of network deployments are the devices at the edge. If that statement seems odd, consider desktop architectures such as twisted-pair Ethernet and the near-ubiquitous Wi-Fi, neither of which made great strides until the technologies were embedded in silicon and offered nearly free on every computer and smartphone sold.

This "edge effect" is amplified by the sheer numbers. There are orders of magnitude more end points than networking devices in most networks. From a cost, deployment, and product life cycle standpoint, it's always been true—until the end points are network-ready, a network architecture is only theory.

These factors apply even more directly to the Internet of Things. There will be literally billions of networked end points, eventually dwarfing the world population traditional Internet to date, as shown in Figure 3-1. But unlike any other network deployment, the IoT end points should be extremely *inexpensive, autonomous,* and mostly *untouched* by human command and control.

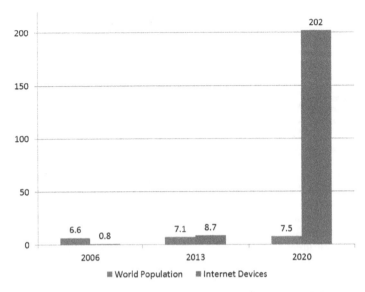

Figure 3-1. *The number of Internet-connected devices exceeded the number of humans in the world around 2009, but the Internet of Things will cause a further exponential increase in the number of devices. Sources: Cisco Systems, International Data Corporation, Population Reference Bureau, U.S. Census World Population Clock, United Nations Department of Economic and Social Affairs*

A World of Different Devices

For many people, the IoT conjures up visions of smartphones, laptops, and similar intelligent, human-oriented devices. But in fact, the statistical bulk of the IoT will consist of relatively simple devices such as pollution sensors, diesel generators, air conditioning systems, building lighting components, and so on. Familiar computing devices, designed for human "high touch," will mostly stay on the traditional Internet, but the Internet of Things will reach far out to the edges of the network to devices that have *never been connected* in the past.

Because these classes of devices have never been connected, there are limited technical models upon which to draw. The connectivity challenges are substantial: there may be limited bandwidth, lossy connections, intermittent links, and power-off periods. In addition, end devices may be mobile or stationary, appearing and disappearing from the network at any time. But the greatest challenges are in the manufacturing, deployment, and management of this vast population of end devices.

As seen in Figure 3-2, IoT devices could be virtually anything that runs on any sort of electricity (or provides or has access to energy such as heat, motion, or light that may be converted to electricity for signaling). IoT-enabled devices may be built in millions of factories and shops across the globe and purchased in millions of different venues. There is no existing (or imagined) technology or business process that could possibly manage this sort of far-flung, uncoordinated global supply chain.

Figure 3-2. *The Internet of Things will include a dizzying variety of end devices, both traditional and obscure*

Intended to be Untended: Some Examples of IoT Systems

Similar to the fish shown in Figure 3-3, IoT devices must act autonomously and independently. It is only from an *external* viewpoint that the devices will appear coordinated. When powered up or otherwise triggered, an IoT device will simply bleat out its data and/or listen for its data. But that sending and receiving will have no bearing on most IoT devices' prime functions.

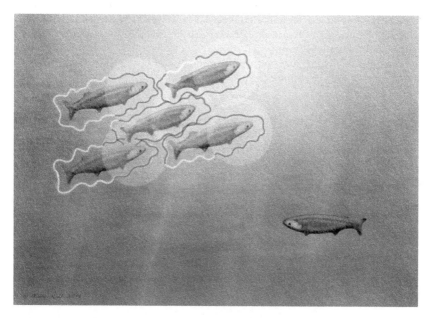

Figure 3-3. *Each fish in a school participates in group movements and behaviors when in contact with others, yet can also exist independently*

43

For example, streetlights will continue turning on and off with the setting and rising of the sun, regardless of whether their status messages are being received somewhere else. Electrical generators will continue cranking out kilowatts without "knowing" whether their terse broadcast reports on lubricant viscosity are being studied. Because networking on the Internet of Things frontier is so lossy, intermittent, and uncertain, it is important not to hamstring the devices with an end-to-end data assurance requirement.

This grows out of the recognition that the Internet of Things will only *indirectly* interact with humans. The vast majority of the communications will be machine-to-machine: generally end devices and integrator functions exchanging information through lossy and intermittent links, typically through relays (propagator nodes). Humans will interact with the integrator functions, retrieving reports or setting parameters that bias the operation of the remote end devices. Interactions that are real time, mission-critical, or human-oriented will mainly continue to use the traditional Internet and other existing "reliable" networking protocols.

Because the vast majority of IoT end devices will be engineered to operate independently of network connectivity, *individual* data messages are completely *uncritical*, as noted earlier. This allows for end devices that cease sending or receiving when powered off, wireless links that are extremely weak or intermittent, solar-powered end devices and other network elements that literally "go dark," and other realities of networking at the edge.

Temporary and Ad Hoc Devices

In fact, an entire class of IoT end devices may exist only transiently as hastily formed networks. Smart disposable "motes" may be deployed for specific purposes, perhaps sending data only for as long as their limited batteries last. A sensor network of this type might be measuring the pressure change of an intruder's footfall, for example, in a temporary protective alarm ring around a facility. The cost, size, and power savings that come from avoiding the overhead of traditional protocols are substantial and will drive these devices and networks to simpler chirp architectures.

Addressing an Uncertain Frontier

One of the major issues to be addressed when contemplating the Internet of Things is how messages to and from end devices may be addressed. This issue was discussed briefly in the preceding chapter and is covered in more detail in Chapter 6, where the three key IoT addressing concepts are explored: self-classification of end device type with external markers, non-guarantee of absolute end device address uniqueness, and end device address derivation from the environment. These basic concepts will allow the uncoordinated "crowd" of end devices to be scaled into a global Internet of Things.

Reliability Through Numbers

Although much of the Internet of Things will be generally predicated on the fact that individual end device connections will be lossy, intermittent, and unreliable, an interesting phenomenon will be the build-up of *reliable* information from a very large number of *individually unreliable* sources.

As an example, consider strain gauge sensors on a highway bridge (see Figure 3-4). It might be desirable to distribute hundreds or thousands of these at many locations on the bridge. Data from the gauges might be collected wirelessly and propagated to an integrator function monitoring the condition of the bridge. But it would be nearly impossible to wire an external power source to each of these sensors. In this case, it might be more practical to make a significant percentage of these devices "solar-powered," energized by either the sun or existing streetlights on the bridge.

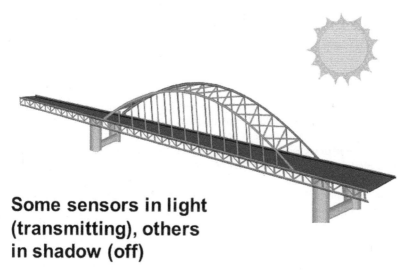

Some sensors in light (transmitting), others in shadow (off)

Figure 3-4. *Thousands of individually unreliable solar–powered strain gauges on a bridge effectively create a single reliable integrated data source*

With the movement of the sun through the sky, different sensors might be illuminated at different times of the day. Some cease to broadcast when in shadow, whereas others begin broadcasting their status when the moving sun casts light on them. Still other sensors' broadcasts might be occasionally interrupted by passing vehicles. However, there will always be hundreds of sensors broadcasting, although no single sensor would be guaranteed to be active at any particular moment.

This is over-provisioning through sheer numbers of end devices, creating a *net* consistency and reliability through integration that would be impractical or prohibitively expensive to provide through highly reliable individual sensors. Similarly, integrator functions might analyze and interpolate information from a variety of unrelated devices to detect events or trends such as a power outage.

Meaning from Many

At this point, it might be worthwhile to briefly consider some examples of how information flowing to and from simple end devices is transported and becomes meaningful in the machine-to-machine world of the Internet of Things (IoT applications will be more thoroughly explored in Chapter 7).

The true power and utility of the IoT comes when vast quantities of data from end devices in the form of short chirps are consolidated, analyzed, and integrated to create "small data" streams of rich information. The resulting small data flows percolate "up" and are converted into big data content. This process will be a key driver for the deployment of the IoT (and was the inspiration for this book). End device chirps that are briefly stored and analyzed at integrator functions will allow the development of perspective and some learning from experience.

End Devices in Dedicated Networks

In the example of streetlights mentioned previously, the on-or-off state and/or OK/Fault status being repeatedly transmitted by small modules within each individual streetlight would be collected via one or more propagator nodes. This communication, in the form of chirps, might be wireless or via very low speed data modulated over electrical power cables. Propagator nodes at central points in the street grid receiving these chirps might ignore repeated transmissions (or reduce the number), bundling the data for forwarding to an integrator function. The propagator node may add contextual information *not available* from the end devices, such as time of day, weather, location, and so on.

The combined data would then typically be encapsulated in an IP packet and forwarded by the propagator node toward an integrator function, as described in Chapter 4. This might be via the traditional Internet, a private wide area network (WAN), or some combination.

The integrator function (typically software operating on a general-purpose processer; see Chapter 5) would be receiving chirp data from streetlights across the city. From these "small data" feeds, a big data perspective could be developed based on analysis and integration over time or as a snapshot of status. Individual streetlight failures or faults beyond a previously defined threshold might cause the integrator function to generate an alarm and report for a human operator's action or might even be integrated with scheduling software to add faulty lights to a repair worker's schedule automatically. In this way, data from relatively "dumb" devices becomes a powerful tool for system management.

Expanding to the World

In the preceding example, the network was fairly sequestered. In fact, this might be desirable for security or other proprietary reasons, and the chirp protocol permits this (see Chapter 6). But tremendous potential uses for chirp data from simple end devices arise in broader settings.

The data from a significant portion of end devices will simply be transmitted with generic public markers (see Chapter 2) that allow it to be interpreted by any integrator function with an understanding of that end device classification and type (moisture sensor versus temperature gauge versus strain gauge, and so on).

One of the key opportunities for new meaning extracted from "small data" is that integrator functions may process a wide range of nominally *unrelated* data sources, as opposed to the fixed end-to-end IP conversations typical of most of the traditional Internet. Integrator functions may perform something of a seemingly variable "random walk"—collecting data in a contingent fashion from a wide variety of end devices *anywhere in the world* based on sampling trends and events. The externally self-classified format of chirps allows all of the elements of the IoT to recognize potentially interesting, but previously unknown, data sources.

There could be huge benefit, for example, from integrating data from thousands of wind speed and direction sensors, barometric pressure gauges, and temperature readings, along with public domain weather reports, to create a highly localized footprint of potential tornado formation. These end-device data sources might not be centrally owned and controlled, but an integrator function could easily seek them out and add them to an ever-growing set of inputs.

The capability to handle both proprietary and generic uses of data creates the need for an IoT architecture and chirp protocol that can be public or private (see Chapter 2). Some data streams from end devices will actually be used by multiple unrelated integrator functions, a factor that propagator nodes must take into account when bundling and forwarding end device chirps (see Chapter 4).

Converting States to Chirps

For a large majority of devices on the Internet of Things, only the bare minimum amount of data will be contributed to these higher-level analyses. As noted previously, a simple On/Off state or an "OK/Fault" condition might be the only useful information that the end device may present. Or a simple voltage differential or current reading will be of interest for a moisture sensor, temperature gauge, or similar device.

For simpler devices such as these, the analog-to-digital interface may likewise be very simple. Ideally, integrated silicon chips will be developed, which simply detect the presence of voltage (or a similar condition) and directly create chirps through very simple logic. This obviates the need for processing, memory, or other computing functions within the majority of end devices.

More importantly, this means that there is no *significant redesign* needed for millions of existing un-networked devices, appliances, and machines. Instead, a simple connection to an existing point in end device wiring or circuitry will provide the information needed to create chirps.

Again, this is a departure from the thinking behind much of the Internet and traditional networks, in which the end devices must have all the functionality needed to create digital data (typically in frames or packets). Instead, much of the IoT will function more along the lines of telemetry, in which states and conditions are coded as simply as possible and then broadcast, as shown in Figure 3-5.

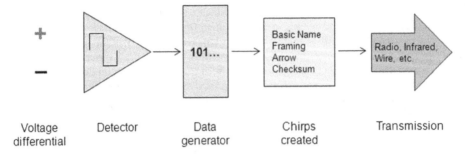

Figure 3-5. *In millions of simple end devices, basic physical states will be converted to chirp payloads. An address, "arrow" of transmission, and checksum are added to this payload to form the complete chirp packet*

It is likely (and perhaps desirable) that some number of standardized chirp formats will be created to handle specific very common states and conditions, such as On/Off, Green/Yellow/Red status states, and so on. A list of suggested potential chirp formats is listed in Appendix A.

"Setting" End Devices

Many of the end device examples explored thus far have been sensors and other devices that will simply broadcast states and conditions and *listen for nothing*. Although this situation may be true for the majority of devices in the Internet of Things, additional billions of devices will be receive-only or bidirectional (sending *and* receiving chirps).

The messages intended for these devices will typically be generated by integrator functions and then propagated "down" (or away from the integrator function) toward end devices by propagator nodes. (Propagator nodes may be directly IP-connected to the general-purpose computer hardware hosting the integrator function, but will more often be reached via the traditional Internet.)

This "direction" of travel is determined by the "arrow" of transmission within the chirp message markers encapsulated in IP, as discussed earlier. Integrator functions will generate these chirps based on human programming, preset alarm conditions, or through routines generated by interactions between integrator functions. At the final destination, the "last" propagator node strips the IP encapsulation and generates native chirps bound for the end device.

As before, many of the targeted end device appliances and actuators will be very simple and thus, the chirps will have very simple payloads. In this way, these end device–bound chirps may resemble the "SetRequest" of Simple Network Management Protocol (SNMP). A key difference with SNMP, however, is that the IoT end device need not acknowledge taking an action directed by the chirp, nor even the reception of an individual chirp. This eliminates a tremendous amount of protocol overhead throughout the network.

As with the end device chirps propagating "up" through the network, these chirps moving "down" will simply be repeated. Because each individual chirp is so tiny, and repeated transmissions may be squelched at the propagator node without clogging wide area connections, the cost of over-provisioning through repetition is small. In applications for which it may be important that the integrator function have some acknowledgment that a chirp was indeed acted upon, bidirectional (send and receive) end devices can be deployed (see Figure 3-6).

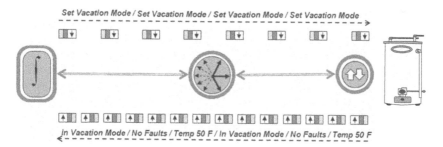

Figure 3-6. *Receive-only and bidirectional end devices receive transmissions from integrator functions via propagator nodes, which handle broadcast bundling and unpacking en route*

Where necessary, these bidirectional end devices may receive chirps (setting a valve position in a process control environment, for example) and also be continually broadcasting chirps that indicate the valve position. In this way, the integrator function need only repeat the command to move the valve—until eventually chirps are received, indicating that the valve is now in the desired position.

The unreliability of any individual transmission suggests that IoT chirp protocols may not be the best choice for real-time and especially critical or dangerous functions. Traditional Internet and other networking protocols will continue to work well in those situations, of course. But for billions and billions of end devices, chirp protocols will provide "good enough" functionality at a vastly reduced cost of bandwidth, processing, memory, and other factors.

The end result may be "neighborhoods" of interest built up by integrator functions consisting of data streams from a combination of IoT chirp protocol end devices (converted to IPv6 by propagators) and more sophisticated end devices communicating via native IPv6. Information extraction and analysis takes place within the integrator function, as described in Chapter 5.

Cornucopia of Connections

Many Internet of Things discussions assume wireless connectivity over traditional networking schemes such as Wi-Fi, Bluetooth, and so on. And it is likely that this will be true, particularly between *propagator nodes* or between *propagator nodes* and *integrator functions*. But connections to end devices may be widely varied—some quite sophisticated and others extremely prosaic. A more detailed look at wireless connectivity will be explored in the extensive sidebar that concludes this chapter titled "Wire-Less vs. Wireless."

Within a residence or enterprise, many end device connections to a collocated propagator node may be via copper media. A few of these may be dedicated wiring, but existing copper wiring infrastructures such as telephone, data, and especially AC power line wiring will often be much more cost-effective. Because a very large number of end devices will be plugged in to AC mains (as will the propagator nodes), there will be a natural opportunity to exploit this in many cases. The amount of IoT data will be low, as noted earlier, so existing AC power line chips and protocols (IEEE 1901 for example) provide more than enough capacity for Internet of Things communications.

With the low data rates and duty cycles of most IoT end devices, other potential existing technologies may also be considered (see Figure 3-7 "Examples of IoT End Devices"). Open-space optical networking techniques such as infrared (IR) may be useful in the home environment, for example. Although IR has mainly been used for remote control of home entertainment and similar devices, networking protocols such as the open-source Linux Infrared Remote Control (LIRC) may present an interesting low-cost alternative for IoT chirp networking (see the "Wire-Less vs. Wireless" sidebar).

Application/ Device	Mode[1]	Chirp Size (bytes)	Frequency/ Minute	Repetition %	Effective Data Rate (kbps)	Typical Transmission[2]
Environmental Sensors (Temperature, vibration, strain, moisture, etc.)	S	4.5	1	90%	<1	Z,B,I,W
Lighting Monitoring and Control	B	6.5	1	90%	<1	P,W
Household Appliances	S	4.5	<1	99%	<1	I,P,Z,B
Inventory / Supply Chain	S	4.5	1	95%	<5	R,Z,W
Video Surveillance (Stand By)[3]	B	4.5	60	99%	5	W,Z,C
"Smart" Signs	R	7.5	1800	90%	22	W,Z,P,I
Home Entertainment Control	B	7.5	600	99%	50	I,W
Process Control (Valves, flow rates, etc.)	B	7.5	60	75%	150	Z,W,C
Industrial Machine Control / Diagnosis	B	7.5	6000	25%	340	W,Z,I,C

[1] S = Send-only device; R = Receive-only device; B = Bidirectional
[2] B = Bluetooth; C = Copper (wired); I = Infrared; P = Power line; R = RFID; W = WiFi; Z = ZigBee. Listed in approximate order of suitability/preference.
[3] In stand by mode, local integrator function is processing video surveillance stream, so only "OK" or "fault status is transmitted by IoT interface. When movement of a particular type is detected locally, device would shift to IP mode in order to transit large frames of full video. Local device may also be triggered to full video mode by command from remote integrator function.

Figure 3-7. A small sampling of IoT End Device types shows tremendous variety in communications types and effective data rates. Note that these are well below typical Internet data rates

No matter which connection techniques are used, chirp messages to and from end devices need only reach a propagator node, where they will be bundled, pruned, and retransmitted as needed to move the traffic through the traditional Internet for connections to integrator functions.

Chirp on a Chip

As noted previously, many Internet of Things end devices will have relatively simple information to share or receive, such as simple states or conditions that may be communicated by the presence or absence of voltage or some other simple "signal." When this is combined with the very simple structure of the IoT chirp packet, the potential exists for extremely cost-effective, mass-produced, integrated silicon chips. These could provide state detection, chirp formation and transmission technology (wired, IR, or radio frequency [RF]) in a single small, inexpensive, and low-power package. (Receive-only and bidirectional integrated devices will also exist with slightly different requirements.)

Development and widespread distribution of these "chirp on a hip" components will be critical to the expansion of the Internet of Things because they will make possible connections to millions of different types of relatively inexpensive devices.

"Chirp chips" might be offered in a variety of tiers, defined by the integration of different functions. Global positioning system (GPS) receivers, electromagnetic position indicators, accelerometers, and other indicators of environmental condition might be interesting potential add-ons, as might radio-frequency identification (RFID), as discussed in the section following). But it's likely that a majority of IoT chirp chips will be relatively simple single-function modules optimized for lowest cost, smallest size, and minimal power consumption. Development and integration of chirp chips is discussed in more detail in Chapter 8.

Aftermarket Options

Integrated chirp chips can become available quickly for new purchases of IoT–ready OEM equipment. But billions of devices already exist that users will desire to have connected to the Internet of Things. For these devices, add-on and aftermarket alternatives need to be developed.

For many simple needs, such as power On/Off or Red/Yellow/Green status, a simple module might plug in between the end device and the AC mains. These might communicate via power line or wireless technologies and would require no software or configuration of the end devices. It can be imagined that these might be built into devices such as power bars and surge protectors. (In this case, the device might also function as a propagator node for all the attached end devices.)

Additional packaging options for aftermarket IoT connections in some applications could include small stand-alone devices based on Universal Serial Bus (USB) and other standardized interfaces, especially those that provide power as part of the interface. Because of the simplicity of the chirp networking protocol, add-on aftermarket devices may be very compact and draw little power. IoT devices will not require the high speeds possible over these interfaces (and their associated costs), but these standards may still be useful due to their wide availability in the market.

RFID Integration in the Internet of Things

For some market participants, interest in the Internet of Things has been *primarily* around the spread of RFID capabilities. RFID is based on a small physical device (a "tag" or "label") that broadcasts stored data, such as a serial number and other information. These devices can be self-powered, but more often are temporarily energized by RF fields generated by the receiving device (the "reader" or "interrogator"). RFID is widely used in inventory tracking and asset management, and its applications are constantly expanding.

Some have viewed each individual tag as an end device in the Internet of Things, and there is certainly some similarity in basic capability between a tag and a simple chirp-enabled end device. But it seems more likely that RFID *readers* will actually function as IoT end devices, perhaps combined with a propagator node.

Because typical RFID tags communicate only identification parameters and have no defined interfaces to other signals (such as voltage presence or differential) within the device to which they are attached, they are significantly more limited than a full chirp end device. But interesting potential exists for combinations of RFID information and chirp data to be received by a propagator node, which could bind the information together before forwarding directly to the integrator function (see Figure 3-8).

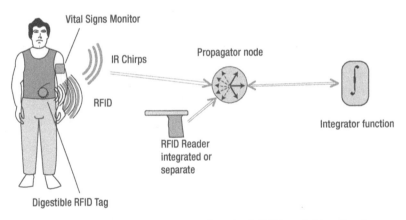

Figure 3-8. *Some applications may combine both RFID and chirp signals to provide both location and state inputs for analysis by an integrator function*

End Devices with Higher Demands

As noted in Chapter 2, relatively simple end devices will predominate numerically within the Internet of Things. But there will still be billions of devices with more demanding communication needs, such as video surveillance systems, teller machines, and telepresence information kiosks, among many others. Many of these have real-time data requirements, high bandwidth needs, and/or human interfaces that make data reliability and bandwidth critical.

For the most part, these devices will therefore remain directly connected to the existing Internet via traditional networking protocols such as TCP/IP. These high-data-need devices will certainly often share the Internet backbone with traffic from propagator nodes comprised of consolidations of chirps to-and from IoT end devices.

But interesting opportunities may exist for combinations of chirp and traditional protocols within a single device. In some cases, simpler status or environmental conditions that are less time-critical might be sent and received via chirps while a high-demand end device is in "StandBy" mode. Then when the device is fully activated (for a human interaction, perhaps), a traditional Internet connection is established for the duration of the high-data-need transaction.

Another potentially interesting application might be to make use of the IoT chirp interface as a back-channel or chording input to the traditional high–bandwidth Internet connection, perhaps in a different frequency or physical domain (see Sidebar "Wire-less vs. Wireless"). Chirp–enabled end devices will likely constitute the vast numerical majority of the Internet of Things, but billions of higher–demand IoT end devices will still comfortably coexist.

The Big Idea: "Small" Data

This chapter has explored the variety of Internet of Things devices in some detail. The only common denominator for IoT-enabled devices may be data—*just a little* for each: tiny squirts and squibs of data—a few bytes reporting moisture content of soil or wind direction or a short instruction to set a valve to a new position. As introduced in Chapter 2 and more fully explained in Chapter 6, these tiny information exchanges are in the form of chirps: simply structured self-classified data packets with minimal overhead.

Individually not impressive or meaningful, these end device chirp data streams become powerful tools when combined and analyzed within integrator functions (see Chapter 5). But first, these myriad chirps must be transported across the Internet of Things networking frontier and (usually) through the traditional Internet. That job falls to the propagator nodes, which will be explored in the next chapter.

WIRE-LESS VS. WIRELESS

Most people picture wireless connectivity when thinking of ways to connect end devices in the IoT. And when thinking of wireless, most consider traditional existing protocols such as Bluetooth, ZigBee, Wi-Fi, and cellular/4G/LTE. Many IoT end devices may indeed be connected using one or more of these protocols (see Figure 3-9), but not only to *these* wireless protocols.

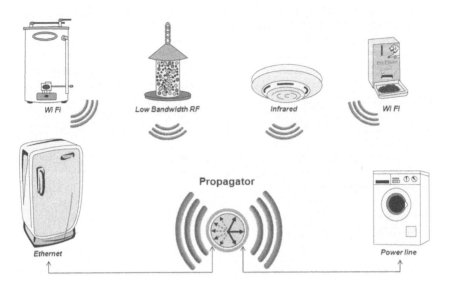

Figure 3-9. *IoT end devices will communicate over various means: optical IR, wireless, power line. Many propagator nodes will be equipped with multiple physical wired and wireless interfaces*

Again, because the total data transmitted to or received from an individual IoT end device is exceedingly small in the vast majority of cases, all those traditional protocols are by definition overkill. Many sensor-type devices will generate only a few bytes of data per hour, for example, and still effectively less after repeated identical transmissions are squelched. Even the lowest ZigBee data rates, for example, are on the order of 20 kilobits per second. This is multiple orders of magnitude greater than the data rate that will be needed for most IoT end devices, although there will be exceptions for other classes of IoT end devices.

Due to these low data rates and duty cycles, the protocol stacks and wireless RF sophistication of standard chips will not be necessary for the typical IoT end device link. Much simpler (read: cheaper) solutions based on simple modulation schemes within existing unlicensed frequencies can therefore be considered.

As noted earlier, these alternatives might include power line, television white spaces frequencies, and open space optical links (IR or visible). The first is obviously potentially attractive for any end device that plugs into AC mains, as long as a propagator node is also plugged into the same building or household somewhere. IR is familiar to most of us in the form of TV and other entertainment system remotes. Wire-less need not be traditional wireless.

Navigating an Already Wireless World

There may be a number of low-cost, unsophisticated wireless modulation schemes developed for the Internet of Things (some possible approaches are suggested in Chapter 6). With such small data rates and duty cycles, very low baud rates are needed, so signaling techniques can be quite simple. It likely goes without saying that virtually all IoT networking must take place in unlicensed frequencies. (It is somewhat contrary to the low cost and simple protocol characteristics of the IoT end device to consider licensed RF bands, although there is nothing in the chirp structure that would preclude this.)

But these new potential wireless IoT solutions will not be deployed in virgin territory—traditional wireless protocols such as Wi-Fi, Bluetooth, and many others are already widely (and unpredictably) deployed using unlicensed RF bands.

Coexistence by Camouflage

Because it will be necessary for IoT wireless signals to coexist with existing protocols such as Wi-Fi, this would seem to demand a traditional wireless protocol stack in every IoT end device and propagator node. Yet this would certainly destroy the low-cost model needed for widespread Internet of Things acceptance and proliferation.

The solution to this problem is based on "hiding in plain sight" within the traditional unlicensed RF environments based on an understanding of their operation. The key will be to exploit time and frequency domain differences. Because IoT chirps are so short and individually uncritical, they may be squeezed into "spaces" that naturally occur when more-sophisticated protocols are in operation (see Figure 3-10).

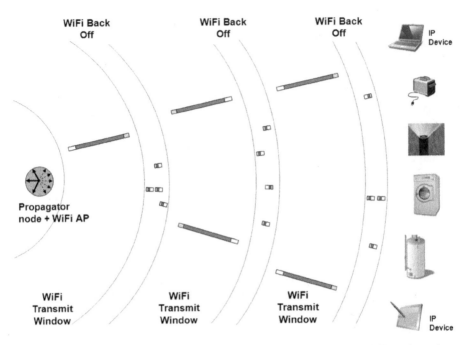

Figure 3-10. IoT chirps "squeezed" between Wi-Fi send-receive cycles, as fully explained in Chapter 6

Collisions? Who Cares?

Selecting Wi-Fi as an example, IoT devices may easily operate within the "quiet time" back-offs inherent in Carrier Sense Multiple Access with Collision Detection (CSMA/CD). IoT end devices simply broadcast or listen for their chirps. Because the chirps are very short, there is little statistical likelihood of one colliding with a Wi-Fi packet, even within a fairly busy Wi-Fi network. And even if one collision does occur, that chirp is individually uncritical, and another will likely get through relatively soon. Randomized timing between chirps will also help avoid any "deadly embrace" problems with devices communicating via traditional wireless protocols (see Chapter 2).

The effect on the Wi-Fi network is also minuscule, again because of the very small chirps and low duty cycle of the typical Internet of Things device. So there is no need to burden IoT end devices or the chirp protocol with any collision detection, avoidance, or recovery capabilities. Propagator nodes, on the other hand, may be the appropriate places to incorporate either a full traditional wireless stack or a "listen for a pause" capability to hold transmissions and avoid unnecessary collisions (see Chapter 4). By bundling and pruning IoT chirp broadcasts, the propagator nodes can be "good citizens" within traditional wireless environments.

"Chording" and Baud Rate

When fully considering all the "wire-less" options such as power line and optical signaling, an interesting set of opportunities is presented. Sending or receiving data in multiple domains simultaneously may increase the baud rate (or decrease the potential for collisions and interference). An individual device might send simple chirps via RF and IR to increase the amount of information transferred while remaining "below the radar" in terms of traditional wireless networking in the same environment.

Like a musical chord, sending multiple pieces of information simultaneously in two frequency domains may offer a potential for very rich communications using the very simple chirp protocol. As more fully described in Chapter 6, this allows a much higher baud (signaling or information) rate than is possible within the bandwidth of a single medium.

CHAPTER 4

■ ■ ■

Building a Web of Things

The massive number of Internet of Things (IoT) end devices described in the preceding chapter will be producing and consuming prodigious amounts of simple data in the form of terse chirps (see Chapter 2). But if these chirps, as described, lack the traditional overhead trappings of well-known protocols such as TCP/IP, how can they be moved across the traditional Internet—or indeed, *across any network at all?*

The majority of IoT end devices will, by design, be cheap, limited in power and memory, and rudimentary. They will not be capable of managing and controlling their own networking as IP devices are expected to do. This networking task will fall to the class of devices called *propagator nodes*. These nodes are technologically a bit more like traditional networking equipment such as switches and routers, but they operate in a more broadly purposed way. IoT chirp-based traffic will be bundled, pruned, converted, and forwarded as necessary to move it throughout the network via a variety of protocols and interfaces. Propagator nodes must include a chirp packet translation into an IP packet because some packets are intended for external consumption. And, of course, the same process will happen in reverse for IP traffic destined for chirp-based end devices.

Most importantly, it will be possible for the function of some classes of propagator nodes to be influenced by agents residing within the integrator functions described in Chapter 5. Biasing the networking activity of the propagator nodes will serve to create software–defined publish/subscribe relationships across the IoT. These logical relationships won't be based on physical network topologies, but on neighborhoods of interest and affinities.

As an example, the affinity group for portable diesel generators operated by a global enterprise may be international. The resulting rollup of chirps through propagator nodes to "small data" to big data creates the power of the emerging Internet of Things (see Figure 4-1).

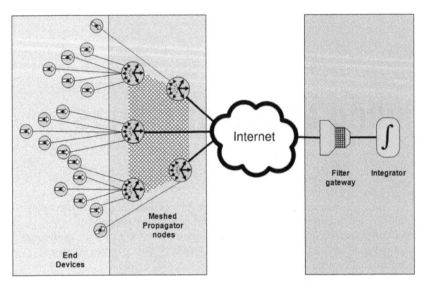

Figure 4-1. *Propagator nodes create the web of the Internet of Things, connecting end devices, other propagator nodes, and integrator functions (some with filter gateways)*

Versatility in Function and Form

Propagator nodes incorporate a number of novel concepts. Their most basic function will be to transport traffic on behalf of a huge range of end devices and other elements, including translation and gateway services to place aggregated chirp messages onto traditional networks such as TCP/IP. They will be expected to build an independent web of interconnection immediately upon power-up, discovering and connecting to nearby end devices, adjacent propagator nodes, and other elements.

In many ways, propagator nodes are the *key building blocks* of the emerging Internet of Things because their functionality allows the vast majority of end devices to remain simple and cheap, even disposable. With propagator nodes in place, IoT networks may be scaled to huge sizes, with each individual propagator node supporting many low-cost chirp–based end devices. Propagator nodes also provide connections to (and through) the traditional Internet to integrator functions in which meaning may be extracted from the "small data" of the end devices.

Architecting Trees and Leaves

The basic principles of the propagator nodes are drawn again from natural phenomena. If the billions of end devices are viewed as the "leaves" of the IoT, the propagator nodes may be seen as the "limbs" and "trunks" that connect them.

The typical tree in nature (see Figure 4-2) is structured: individual leaves do not connect to one another directly because *they have nothing of value for one another*. Instead, the branches, limbs, and trunks of the tree serve to bring water and nutrients to the leaves and carry manufactured food from leaves to roots. From tiny shrubs to mighty redwoods, trees scale because they are structured based on this basic flow: the input and output of untold millions of end points is organized for maximum efficiency.

Figure 4-2. *Trees are inherently structured: no leaf connects directly to another. Instead, flows are organized through trunks, limbs, and branches. Internet of Things traffic will be similarly structured to present data only where it has meaning. Nature's arteries—rivers, trees, and so on—generally tend to be self-forming, dynamic, recursive tree-like topologies. Obviously, there is no computing resource available in nature to calculate a graph-based organization. Routing is simpler within this organic structure of recursive branching. (See the "Why Trees Scale" sidebar)*

SIDEBAR: WHY TREES SCALE

A structured tree-like network (which can be referred to as "Order n" [O(n)]), is linear with tree depth and therefore scales even in very large sizes. It scales because Moore's Law, which is also linear, is useful only when applied to counteract degradation effects, is also O(n). Anything more, for example, O(n-squared) systems, simply cannot scale with linear efficiency improvements and compensations. In nature, such systems would eventually reach extinction because of natural selection, which through trial and error over generations, would prune inefficient transport of nutrients from the root to leaves and vice versa (up and down the tree's network). Hence, O(n) systems prevail in nature, in large part because they are inherently efficient—and thus scalable.

> The flow of data in an IoT context is also inherently hierarchical and tree-like. At the root, there is the tree trunk and its more-focused flow. The tree trunk then again branches out into roots and tendrils.
>
> At the other end, branches assimilate small data emanating from the "leaves" (end devices). The entire process of how small data (from a myriad of end devices) is assimilated, pruned, modified, and then forwarded is hierarchical in the IoT, just as in trees.
>
> One can imagine the two tree-like structures (roots and branches) coalescing into one central location: the trunk. This is where the big data services, such as integrator functions, reside.

No doubt other types of nutrient transport technologies exist in nature in smaller plants, but none has demonstrated the majestic scaling seen in trees. For the same reasons, tree-like structured networks will prevail at the edges of the IoT. Unlike a natural "tree," human networks, with their unlimited peer-to-peer interactions, create the need for constant computing and updating for additions and perturbations. This is the major driver for using networking protocols (such as TCP/IP) with traditional Internet end points such as smartphones and PCs.

On Behalf of Chirps at the Edge

But the majority of end devices in the Internet of Things will communicate via the lightweight chirp protocol, as described in Chapter 3. chirp protocol includes only minimal addressing and error detection (Chapter 2). Therefore, global naming, full TCP/IP formatting, and protocol services must be applied elsewhere if the data is to pass to-and-from end devices.

Propagator nodes provide these services on behalf of end devices, so at least one propagator node must be in the communications path of any chirp end device so that the simple chirp transmissions may be transformed in order to be carried over the Internet and then interpreted by an integrator function (each of which are based on traditional TCP/IP). Propagator nodes perform this important function of grooming traffic for transmission to-and-from the traditional Internet and other TCP/IP networks.

Because they link the end-device chirp world and the broader IP-based network, propagator nodes will often be equipped with multiple wired and/or wireless interfaces. The "range" of a propagator node depends on the type of connections it has to its end devices. In a home network example, a propagator node might have two wireless interfaces (one to communicate with chirp–based end devices using infrared LEDS and a second IP-based connection such as Wi-Fi) to communicate with a standard 802.11 access point.

Isolating and Securing the Edge

As described here, the propagator nodes' prime function is linking the chirp–based end-devices to one or more integrator functions. These integrator functions are reached via the IP network, with the propagator nodes performing the bridging between the chirp subnetwork and its IP parent network. Without accredited propagator nodes as the "middle man," chirp devices are unreachable from the IP side of the network. This is intentional: chirp devices become inherently secure if they are invisible in the IP addressable space of devices. Propagators are thus essential to providing the final level of control of mission-critical remote systems.

Autonomy and Coordination

With no practical way for the Internet of Things to be engineered in an overall top-down way (maximally efficient) nor to be effectively over-provisioned to the edge (minimally efficient), propagator nodes must be designed to independently develop *reasonably* efficient network architectures. This will require a balance between autonomy and cooperation that may be provided only by the use of robot-like intelligence distributed in each propagator node.

We'll examine first the general techniques used by all propagator nodes in creating the IoT architecture and then later explore different classes and modes of operation in their specific applications.

Upon power-up, each propagator node will assess its surroundings for possible connections to other IoT devices, including the type, characteristics, and functionality of adjacent communicating elements. These connections might be end devices, other propagator nodes, or integrator functions (and their associated filter gateways, as discussed in Chapter 5). Depending on the specific interfaces available (discussed below), these connections can be wired or wireless, via the traditional Internet, or even internal to the propagator node depending on packaging choices (see below). This same start-up procedure is repeated if a primary networking link is lost.

In some ways, this is similar to the discovery mechanisms used by other networking devices such as switches and routers. But unlike most IP-based devices, the overall structure of the network is "bottom-up," with each individual node having the power to create a structured (loop-free) path through negotiation with its peers. This is distinct from many traditional networks, which are engineered top-down using the capabilities designed into IP for the task (and shouldering the IP overhead to do so).

Structuring a Networking Path

The propagator node begins its startup by looking for a path to one or more integrator functions. Occasionally, this will be a direct wired or wireless connection (perhaps through the integrator functions' associated filter gateway). But in the majority of cases, there will be no directly connected integrator function. (Integrator functions are always connected via IP, so at least one propagator node in the path must be equipped to convert traffic from chirp to IP and back, as described below.)

Where there is no locally connected integrator function, the propagator node will exchange information with any other propagator node that is connected, wirelessly or wired. Each propagator node will build its own table of adjacencies, a logical network tree, so this information may be shared to permit the independent intelligence in each propagator node to determine a reasonably efficient path to one or more integrator functions.

Routes are weighted based on the number of "hops" (node-to-node connections) required to reach the integrator functions and may also consider adjacent propagator node loading and bandwidth available. Trade-offs are made between taking a more reliable but circuitous (more hops) route to the destination integrator function versus a more direct, but more loaded, connection. Similar to cars in rush-hour traffic, freeways are less efficient when crowded than a more circuitous city street route.

As seen in Figure 4-3, some propagator nodes may discover direct paths to the Internet (top node), which will *usually* provide the best path to one or more integrator nodes using an IP connection. But many propagator nodes will not have a direct path to the Internet and will instead connect via adjacent propagator nodes using either chirp or IP protocols.

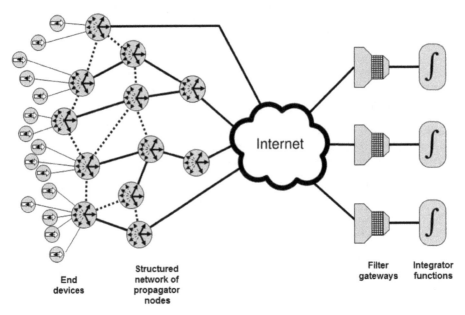

Figure 4-3. When functioning generically, individual propagator nodes consider path information shared by adjacent nodes in building a reasonably efficient path to one or more integrator functions

Many alternate paths may also be discovered (dotted lines); each individual propagator node will choose only one primary connection based on the information on speed, congestion, number of hops (node-to-node connections), past reliability, and so on provided by adjacent propagator nodes via housekeeping frames (see below). Alternate paths are kept in reserve in case of path or intermediate node failure, or significant speed/quality changes.

The establishment of a path to one or more integrator functions defines the "arrow" of transmission introduced in Chapter 2 and described more fully in Chapter 6. The path definition allows the propagator node to make the basic routing decisions for traffic destined for end devices versus integrator functions. This tree-based calculation maps to both the physical and the logical subnetwork of chirp devices.

The "arrow" may be loosely thought of as an overall *inherent* direction similar to upstream/uphill or downstream/downhill flows in nature. The task of the propagator nodes is to organize themselves to provide efficient flows in both directions, possibly through alternative paths.

The basic routing algorithm will also be weighted to make some specific decisions, such as preferring a wired connection to wireless if other factors are equal, but will also take note of path quality information from adjacent nodes (reliability over time, and so on).

Path decisions are revisited periodically to encompass perturbations and failures, the addition of new network elements, and updated path quality information. With each propagator node and transmission path added to the network, the immediately adjacent propagator nodes will reexamine their path analysis in order to maintain reasonably efficient paths to one or more integrator functions. Propagator nodes also perform a fresh search of possible adjacent nodes at regular intervals to discover potential new paths and new adjacent propagator nodes.

Structuring a Tree—with Redundancy

In a logical view, the typical Internet of Things relationship will be one or a few integrator functions to thousands or millions of end devices. Given the basic premise that only a branching tree may scale to the huge network size inherent in the Internet of Things, the most efficient overall network topology will thus take the form of a tree with limbs and branches at the high-volume "end device" edge of the network.

But there may be many possible paths discovered by each propagator node as it examines the data provided by adjacent propagator nodes. Without an overall computation of the entire network structure (which would be impossible), some method is required to avoid circular routing paths.

Individual propagator nodes create the necessary tree structure as they populate their routing tables with potential paths. Alternate possible paths that are deemed less desirable due to hop count, bandwidth, or quality history are noted but not activated. Instead, they are retained as potential backup paths if the primary chosen path is lost for a significant amount of time, as shown in Figure 4-4.

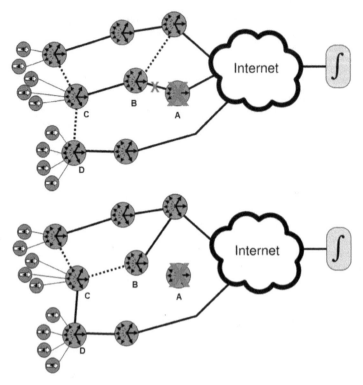

Figure 4-4. *Alternate paths that are not in use are maintained in propagator node routing tables for use as alternate paths in case of the failure of a data path or adjacent propagator node. In the example above, a failure at Node A causes Node B to activate a back-up route. But Node C makes its own routing decision and may select Node D as a better choice rather than following its previous "parent." The tree structure (no loops) is maintained in the new routing*

In this way, failover to an alternate path may take place reasonably quickly. Routing path data will be regularly "aged out" of the table as required to keep the information on possible redundant paths as current as possible.

Housekeeping

As noted previously, a small amount of link and path quality data must be regularly exchanged between adjacent nodes as a housekeeping message. In order for this to be reasonably efficient, there are two classes of information exchanged, circulated to all known adjacent nodes.

A "full" housekeeping message contains a complete "snapshot" of information on adjacencies and link paths from each node and is generated and broadcast every 60 to 600 seconds. The full housekeeping message would typically be in the range of 1,000 to 2,000 bytes of data. A "light" housekeeping packet includes only changes from the last "full" update and is generated every 15 to 60 seconds, with a size of 10 to 100 bytes of data.

When there have been no changes, this lightweight packet provides a confirmation to adjacent propagator nodes that the broadcasting propagator node is still functioning.

This means that a new propagator node joining the network must wait for a full housekeeping packet before it can complete its path analysis. But even light housekeeping packets provide useful information by indicating the presence of an adjacent propagator node.

Propagator nodes also maintain tables of the identities of attached end devices and report this information to adjacent nodes via full housekeeping packets.

By Any Means

To this point, there has been no distinction made between the different possible networking protocols used for connections between propagator nodes. This has been intentional, as the general network decision-making is the same. Individual link paths are abstracted as different channels, each with its own weighting, see Figure 4-5. In some cases, the link between propagator nodes may be simple chirp protocols; in other cases, full TCP/IP connections via the traditional Internet.

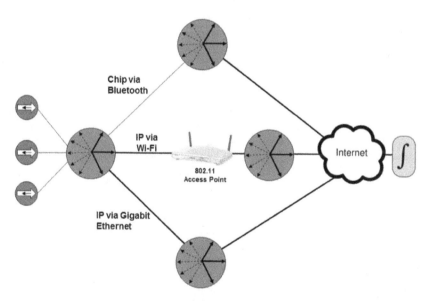

Figure 4-5. *Propagator nodes treat every possible link type as a different channel, abstracting the route-decision algorithm from specific protocols. Although operating at vastly different speeds, any of the three links from the propagator node at left could be used as a path to an integrator function via the Internet*

In the latter case, the propagator node will typically use Dynamic Host Configuration Protocol (DHCP) so that it can communicate on the network using the IP. Housekeeping packets between propagator nodes will be encapsulated within TCP/IP (along with all the other traffic via that path, of course). As noted before, chirp protocol communication and the associated end devices are isolated "behind" the propagator node network.

Take Out the Thrash

As with any networking system, it is critical to avoid hysteresis and thrashing in the structure of the networking "tree" formed by propagator nodes that might be caused by rapidly changing or inconsistent path quality. This might be caused by degraded or failed wireless links or the loss of one or more propagator nodes due to power outage or equipment failure. These changes in the availability and/or quality of individual links or nodes will "ripple" through adjacent propagator nodes in the path of the logically structured tree. The ability to manage such perturbations is especially critical in the Internet of Things, where communications at the edge of the network may be intermittent and of low quality as a matter of course.

Fortunately, the generally low data rates and completely uncritical nature of any individual transmission of the Internet of Things (see Chapter 2) means that a relatively high damping may be applied to the path determination algorithms. The goal is only reasonable efficiency, not overall network optimization, again because of the unique nature of the traffic on the IoT and the capability of propagator nodes to monitor, prune, and tune overall network performance. The tree-based topology ensures that individual propagator node decisions to route via one propagator node versus another are driven by the overall tree route efficiency. This is covered in more depth in Chapter 6.

The Power of Bias and the Role of the Integrator Function

The previous general description includes the basic network capabilities common to all propagator nodes. But the greatest power of the Internet of Things will come as integrator functions create vast networks of data streams encompassing very large numbers of end devices. Based on "neighborhoods of interest" and "affinity" (fully described in Chapter 5), the tiny chirps of end devices are aggregated into small data streams at the propagator nodes, coalesced into big data, and then transformed into useful information at the integrator functions.

This is the essence of the publish/subscribe model in the context of the Internet of Things: the end devices simply broadcast data in the form of chirps without any knowledge of how or where this data will be used. The integrator functions independently create neighborhoods of interest by selecting from available data sources.

For efficiency's sake, it makes sense for the path this data takes, from end device through propagator nodes and on toward the integrator functions, to be actively and intelligently managed as a publish/subscribe model defined by the integrator functions.

This will be achieved by a publishing agent within some classes of propagator nodes (Figure 4-6). This publishing agent may be biased by instructions from one or more integrator nodes to create specific data paths and/or bundle chirp data in specific combinations. Because chirp data is inherently self-classified by external markers, publishing agents may act upon the data by type.

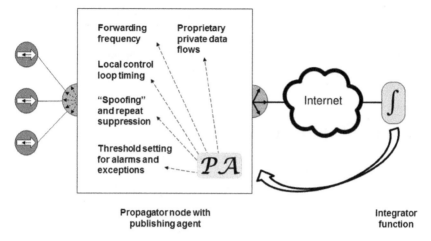

Propagator node with
publishing agent

Integrator
function

Figure 4-6. To unlock the full power of the Internet of Things, some classes of propagator node will contain a publishing agent that may be directed by one or more integrator functions to create and modify a publish/subscribe data flow

Because most of the data paths in these types of relationships will be via the traditional Internet, TCP/IP protocols will be the norm for links from the propagator nodes to integrator functions. This is a logical accompaniment to the publish/subscribe model, in which the end points are known.

The relationship between the integrator function and publishing agent in the propagator node will often be proprietary. For example, a particular manufacturer may provision a publishing agent in its own line of propagator nodes for specific use with that same manufacturer's integrator function. Although the propagator node might also function generically for other Internet of Things traffic, data from specific types of end devices might preferentially be packed for publishing to that integrator function.

Bias and Influence

Although the proprietary relationships described previously will be more typical, there may also be situations where the data being aggregated by a particular propagator node is required by multiple integrator functions for multiple applications or users, either simultaneously or over time.

The publishing agent will respond to the most recent and most frequent biasing messages from the integrator functions. More frequent and more recent messages will reinforce an existing publish/subscribe relationship, while less-frequent messages will allow the propagator node to revert to a more generic function of simply propagating all chirps promiscuously. Over time, this means that the publish/subscribe model may shift organically in response to changing needs, seasonality, events, and so on.

One could consider the example of transit bus schedules, in which routes and timing are managed centrally. The transportation of chirp–cased small data is similarly driven by the needs of the big data centers and their subscription preferences for the published small data flows. Setting up the schedules and routes is managed from the top down because bias and interest in some chirp streams change when and how chirps are transmitted.

In effect, the relationship of integrator functions and propagator nodes is a form of software-defined networking driven by publish/subscribe agents operating on behalf of integrator functions—completely independent of the physical network topology. This is more fully described in Chapter 5.

Degrees of Functionality

Varying end user requirements and applications will create the need for multiple classes of propagator nodes (see Figure 4-7). Specific types of propagator nodes will contain a publishing agent that may interact with one or more integrator functions. But other classes of propagator nodes will function more generically.

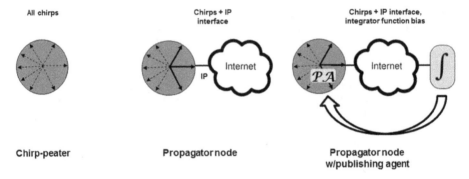

Figure 4-7. *Depending on the application, differing levels of propagator node functionality will be needed. Data forwarding is more selective moving left to right*

The most basic class of propagator node might be dubbed the "chirp-peater." Aggregated chirp messages for associated end devices are simply packaged and forwarded to one or more adjacent propagator nodes. This simplest class of propagator nodes will include only chirp interfaces, with another nearby propagator node providing TCP/IP gateways and other functions. One version of this class of propagator nodes may be designed to act as a client to an 802.11 access point for easiest integration of chirp protocol end devices into existing wireless networks in the home and office.

More powerful propagator nodes will be equipped with more sophisticated networking protocol stacks, gateways, and interfaces. Key among these will be TCP/IP gateways that permit routing through the Internet. They can be used for connections to integrator functions, for propagator-node-to-propagator-node links, and for integration of end devices that include a full TCP/IP stack. Some percentage of these fully featured devices will include the publishing agent described previously, which may often be part of a proprietary publish/subscribe overlay on the general propagator node functions.

But many propagator nodes will be deployed in a "promiscuous broadcast" mode, transporting all received traffic based on the "arrow" of transmission contained within the chirp packet markers. Although there will be little or no routing specificity in these transmissions, there *will* typically be management of repeated transmission, broadcast trimming and pruning, and so on (described below and more fully in Chapter 6). Propagator nodes deployed in this mode will transport IoT traffic on behalf of any device and may become an important part of public and open source Internet of Things networks of unprecedented scope that have yet to be fully conceptualized.

Aggregating End Points

The other "side" of the propagator node consists of the array of interfaces facing the chirp-equipped end devices. Here too, propagator nodes will have many different physical and logical interfaces, both wired and wireless. Beyond traditional interfaces such as Ethernet, 802.11 Wi-Fi, Bluetooth, and so on, wide usage of optical interfaces such as infrared and other low-cost alternatives such as power line networking will also be found, as seen in Figure 4-8.

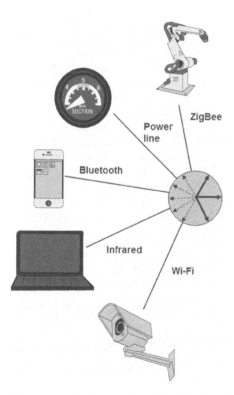

Figure 4-8. *A wide variety of end device physical interfaces may be accommodated, all communicating via chirp protocols. Propagator nodes will vary in the type and number of interfaces provided based on user requirements*

Whatever the mix of physical interfaces chosen, the chirp will be the fundamental data interface to most end devices. As noted in Chapter 3, there will be many bidirectional end devices, but the majority will likely be primarily or solely simplex, whether transmit or receive. In addition, as discussed before, many of these devices will have relatively low information rates, whatever their transmission rate. In other words, in many cases there will be a tremendous amount of repetition in the data that is sent or received by end user devices, which is the subject of the next section.

Dumping the Dupes

Devices such as pressure and moisture sensors, depending on the granularity of their measurement capabilities, will likely send the same value repeatedly for long periods of time. In the reverse direction, the valve servo in a process control application may remain in the same position for extended durations. So in these cases, there will be repeated reports or commands of identical data being sent.

More sophisticated propagator nodes will be designed with consideration of this excessive duplication of data that will likely be a hallmark of much of the Internet of Things. Data streams will be monitored and duplicate messages deleted and/or spoofed locally to avoid transmitting unneeded repetitive data to-and-from integrator functions.

Especially for those propagator nodes equipped with an internal publishing agent (described previously), the integrator functions may bias the propagator node to transmit only data indicative of readings that exceed certain thresholds in frequency and/or value.

These propagator node capabilities will limit the amount of IoT data to be transmitted. Even though individual chirps are much more compact and efficient than traditional protocols such as TCP/IP, the massive scale of the Internet of Things makes it critical to limit inconsequential repeated data wherever possible. Techniques to be used are more fully described in Chapter 6.

Loading the Bus: The Propagator Node Transit System

Another key function of propagator nodes will be managing and packaging broadcasts at all levels in the network. Lightweight chirps are ideal for the typical low-speed, low-duty cycle communication between end device and propagator node in the IoT. But if each of these chirps is then enveloped individually in a (relatively) huge TCP/IP packet before forwarding to the next propagator node, all efficiencies are lost.

Instead, propagator nodes will use their knowledge of adjacencies and routes through the network to accumulate chirps that may be efficiently forwarded *together* to the next propagator node (as noted previously, repeated chirps may be deleted or spoofed). At each successive node, these "buses" may be unloaded, some packets removed and others added, and then forwarded again, as shown in Figure 4-9.

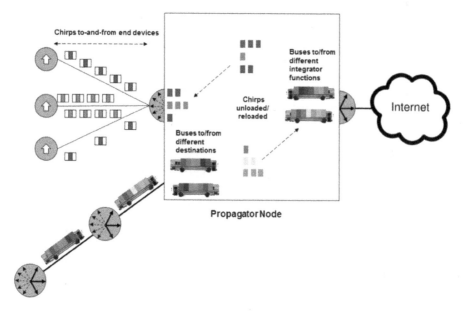

Figure 4-9. *For maximum efficiency in communication between propagator nodes, a "bus" departs periodically for adjacent propagator nodes or integrator functions via the traditional Internet or other data paths. Bus size is optimized for the particular path. At an intermediate propagator node, "buses" are reexamined, local traffic removed, and additional onward traffic added as appropriate*

This process of consolidation, pruning, and forwarding adds a delay at every intermediate point, both for processing time and a lag as the propagator node waits for a certain period to fill the "bus" as much as possible before transmitting. But in the world of the Internet of Things, these delays will have no impact on the usefulness of the data.

Bus sizes will be chosen based on the characteristics of the channel over which they will be forwarded. For TCP/IP paths, propagator nodes will attempt to fill out a packet before forwarding. For other paths, the "bus" size will also be adjusted for maximum efficiency.

Where the publishing agents in specific propagator nodes have been biased by an integrator function, these routing preferences and (typically) TCP/IP packet characteristics will take precedence over the more mechanical process defined above.

Weathering the Storms

In any network capable of broadcasts, the potential for debilitating broadcast storms is present. Propagator nodes inherently limit broadcast storm propagation through the overall tree-like structure, deletion of repeated data, and consolidation and pruning of broadcasts to and from end devices.

Detailed descriptions of the propagator node techniques used for managing traffic to-and-from end devices are found in Chapter 6.

Dodging the Collisions

As noted in Chapter 2, the simplified chirp protocols incorporate no error checking, collision detection, or collision avoidance. Instead, simple randomization schemes and variable back-offs ensure that the tiny chirps may be squeezed between other transmission in the same wireless spectrum without the risk of a "deadly embrace." Propagator nodes use these same techniques on the chirp interfaces.

What's in a Name?

A key premise of the emerging architecture for the Internet of Things is that end user devices are burdened with only the very simple chirp protocol. As described in Chapter 2, the names applied by end devices in chirps are incomplete and likely will not be unique across the network.

This limitation would be problematic if chirps were simply transmitted as-is to other devices. But propagator nodes provide the additional context and addressing specificity needed to create unique addressing, as shown in Figure 4-10. These details are developed from the routing table adjacencies and other information available to the propagator node, as described in detail in Chapter 6.

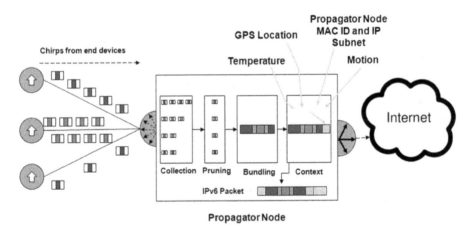

Figure 4-10. *As chirps are bundled within propagator nodes, additional location, addressing, protocol, and other information is added*

Propagator nodes may then "publish" these small data streams onward toward the appropriate integrator function via the propagator node network or, with addition of the appropriate IPv6 encapsulation, directly via the traditional Internet.

For data whose "arrow" points toward the end device, the procedure is reversed: headers and formatting needed for routing to the target propagator node are stripped by that device, and only a lightweight chirp is transmitted to the end device using that device's simple non-unique address.

Packaging Options

There will be many packaging combinations of end devices, propagator nodes, integrator functions, and so on. A particularly interesting combination may be a propagator node with an on-board specialized integrator function. An example of this combination might be designed for local analysis of video surveillance and alarm data, with only exceptions and unusual combinations of data being propagated up to a central site.

Propagator nodes will certainly be packaged with existing types of networking and home entertainment equipment, including routers, Wi-Fi access points, LAN switches, set-top boxes, and so on. There will also be packaging options with nontraditional devices such as smart meters, vehicles, televisions, air conditioning and lighting equipment, and various household appliances as shown in Figure 4-11. Propagator nodes may require little or no human intervention and may be unobtrusively packaged as a wall wart or in other inconspicuous form factors.

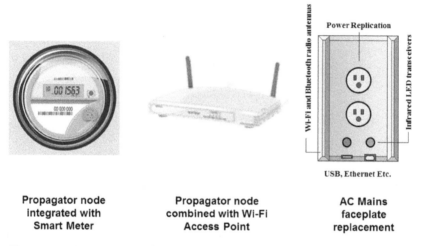

| Propagator node integrated with Smart Meter | Propagator node combined with Wi-Fi Access Point | AC Mains faceplate replacement |

Figure 4-11. *Propagator nodes will be available in many form factors and in combination with other devices from the IoT, including end devices and integrator functions*

Commercial environments will find propagator nodes (often in combination with end devices) in manufacturing equipment, process control devices, vehicles, and many more.

Although it is likely that some instantiations of the propagator node will be software-only on platforms such as smartphones, tablets, or PCs, these devices typically will have two limitations: insufficient number and variety of interfaces for connecting to end user devices and the transient nature of their location.

Packaging options and example network configurations are further discussed in Chapter 7.

Building Blocks of the IoT

Propagator nodes truly are the fundamental components of the tree-like structure of the emerging architecture for the Internet of Things. Propagator nodes create reasonably efficient networks for the transport of IoT data while controlling broadcasts and eliminating unnecessary repetitive data. They make possible the conversion of the lightweight protocols at the edge of the network to the more robust protocols demanded in the traditional Internet and elsewhere.

The next chapter will explore the "business end" of all these data flows: the human-facing integrator functions.

CHAPTER 5

■ ■ ■

Small Data, Big Data, and Human Interaction

Integrator functions are the location in the Internet of Things (IoT) where the chirps from hundreds to millions of end devices are analyzed and acted upon. Integrator functions also send their own chirps to get information or to set values at devices—of course, these chirps' transmission arrow (refer to Chapter 3) is pointed *toward* devices. Integrator functions may also incorporate a variety of *external* inputs, from big data to social networking trends to weather reports.

Integrator functions serve as the human interface to the IoT. As such, they will be designed to reduce the unfathomably large amounts of data collected over a period of time to a simpler set of alarms, exceptions, and other reports for consumption by humans (or computers). In the other direction, they will be used to manage the IoT by biasing agents within propagator nodes (refer to Chapter 3) and other devices to operate within certain desired parameters.

In this way, integrator functions create the publish/subscribe network that extracts meaning from the Internet of Things. Integrator functions define neighborhoods and affinities that are the key relationships within the IoT, regardless of geographical location or network topologies (see Figure 5-1).

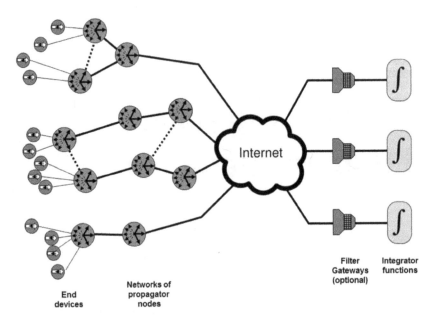

Figure 5-1. *Integrator functions are logically at the center of the Internet of Things publish/subscribe network, although their physical location is unrestricted*

Using simple concepts such as "cluster" and "avoid," integrated scheduling and decision-making processes within the integrator functions will allow much of the IoT to operate transparently and without human intervention. Only a single integrator function might be needed for an average household, operating on a smartphone, computer, or home entertainment device. Or the integrator function could be distributed and scaled up on racks of far-flung processors for a huge global enterprise, tracking and managing energy usage across a corporation, for example.

The "Brains" of the IoT

The most typical form of integrator function consists of specialized software operating on standard off-the-shelf computing platforms. Requirements for the integrator function are for the most part similar to those of other computing-intensive applications: processor horsepower and memory.

For maximum economy of scale and full exploitation of Moore's Law over time, widely deployed computing platforms and operating systems will likely be the primary targets for integrator function software development. Computing power and memory will be commensurate with the amount of data to be analyzed and/or the quantity and sophistication of the end devices to be controlled. Low-end home automation may be achieved with a smartphone and an appropriate app, while monitoring an extensive global process control enterprise (such as oil production) might require clusters of high-end processors with redundancy and fail-over capabilities (see Figure 5-2.).

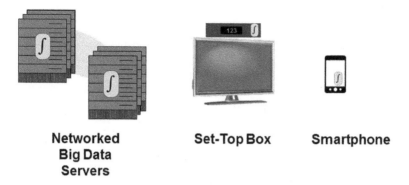

Networked Big Data Servers   **Set-Top Box**   **Smartphone**

Figure 5-2. *Integrator functions may be hosted on a very wide range of general-purpose and broadly deployed computers and devices*

Fortunately, the processor and software development paths (clustered processors, Apache Hadoop distributed file systems, converged network adapters, solid-state storage, etc.) that support expanding big data applications will seamlessly incorporate the emerging Internet of Things integrator function as well.

For Once, IP Makes Sense

To minimize cost and complexity, chirp protocols have been described in the preceding chapters for the end devices that will form the vast numerical majority of the Internet of Things. As explained, these simple protocols will not be sufficient (or even formatted) for transport across the global Internet. Instead, data streams to and from end devices will pass through one or more propagator nodes before routing via standard IP over the Internet (or rarely, a private IP network or VPN) to one or more integrator functions.

The logic in requiring an IP-capable propagator node in the data path now becomes obvious: at the lower networking protocol levels, integrator functions may simply rely on standard IP networking capabilities *already* deployed in typical operating systems with a simple connection made to the Internet via Gigabit Ethernet or other existing and widely deployed interfaces. The architecture of the integrator function builds on many of the same principles as cloud-based computing and will benefit from investments and developers in cloud-based servers and Internet backbone build-outs.

IP-based integrator functions also directly incorporate legacy Internet of Things devices that offer only IP interfaces. This creates an easy transition to the emerging IoT architecture for millions of already installed sensors and actuators, as well as for higher-performance end devices that will remain IP. Integrator functions can also interact directly with millions of existing web-based data feeds and services, creating richer meaning when these sources are combined with IoT data streams.

The downside to this approach of leveraging the global Internet and commercial systems is that very large data streams and busy network interfaces could bog down a general-purpose processor. For this reason, filter gateways (see following) may often be deployed as a specialized appliance to forward only meaningful data (as determined by the integrator function). This ensures that the computing resources of the integrator function may be focused purely on analysis and control tasks.

Extracting the Streams

But as described in preceding chapters and more fully in Chapter 6, the majority of Internet of Things data bundled and forwarded by propagator nodes consists of a distilled stream of chirps encapsulated in IP, not wasteful discrete IP packets for each end device (see Figure 5-3). An internal gateway process within the integrator function must unpack and identify chirp streams for action.

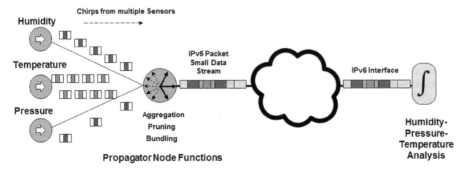

Figure 5-3. *Chirps from IoT end devices are aggregated, pruned, and bundled in the propagator node network; then encapsulated in IP for delivery to an integrator function as a small data "stream" from which the data may be analyzed. A similar process operates in reverse to deliver data to end devices*

Similarly, for outbound traffic such as control packets to valves in a process control application, the integrator function will package chirps within IP packets in a form understandable by the propagator node network. Along their path, these packets will be disassembled, reassembled, repeated, and pruned as necessary to reach the target end devices.

Analysis and Control

With the various inbound streams identified and separated, the integrator function may begin forming a "picture" of the *neighborhood* in which it is interested. Neighborhoods are described more fully later, but they basically consist of a universe of devices that correspond to the type, location, activity level, and so on that the integrator function has been programmed to seek out. For inbound streams, the end devices are *publishing* data to which the integrator function *subscribes*. (And the inverse is true for end devices controlled by the integrator function.)

But the integrator function is not *necessarily* limited to a hard-coded set of specific locations or device types in forming the publish/subscribe neighborhood. A broader set of possible relationships, called *affinities*, may allow an integrator function to create a neighborhood from unrelated end device streams if an interesting or recurring pattern is noted among devices (see Figure 5-4).

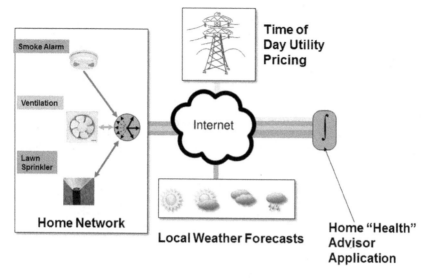

Figure 5-4. *Integrator functions subscribe to interesting data streams published by IoT end devices. An integrator function's "neighborhood" may span the globe. "Affinities" with other potentially associated data may also be exploited to create richer information*

This capability begins to tap into the tremendous potential of the Internet of Things to create useful information and meaning by collecting information from a wide array of devices, many of which may have been deployed *by other entities for other purposes*. To fully appreciate the potential, it is necessary to look beyond traditional end-to-end networks and even software-defined networking concepts to examine the development of meaning from a wide array of sources. One way to appreciate this concept is through a neighborhood analogy.

Chirps to "Small Data" to Big Data: An Example

The build-up of data from many devices is similar in some ways to the build-up of musical tunes from discrete notes. Individually, an isolated note offers no musical information (emotional content, beauty, etc. as determined by a listener). But a series of notes from many sources (the instruments in a symphony, for example) form tunes that human listeners may interpret.

Similarly, chirp sequences (in parallel or serial flow) form "tunes" after a fashion. The chirp stream "tune" is used as a signature pattern or a data payload. Or a concatenated and encrypted version of both (see Chapter 6) where encryption includes delayed transmission as in syncopation. Multiple tunes are really a jumbled version of hidden information, where even the silence may have meaning, known only to intended receivers.

Although humans can hear a birdsong, the chirp sequence "meaning" is known only to the birds. Although humans hear the tune, they cannot decipher it (see Figure 5-5). Birdsong signatures ("blue jay") and payload ("intruder") are both tunes, so it is unclear where one sort of tune melds into another. Hence, humans can hear all the myriad bird conversations in the park and yet understand none—they do not have a decoder key.

Figure 5-5. *The movement of the neighborhood cat sets off "alarms" in a number of "sensor devices" (birds). A human observer may correlate information from multiple senses and understand what is taking place*

Bird chirps respond to changes in the environment. For example, a cat walks through the park. Human eyes can follow it, noticing how the chirps follow the cat's motion as it moves from one tree to another. Chirp tunes will change both in the sequence of tones and their intensity. An observer may be able to discern activities common to the same consensual domain by matching patterns in two *different* sensor domains (eyes and ears) and "putting two and two together." Multiple sensor fusion (eyes and ears, in this case) drives the human inference engine.

Over the course of a month, the cat may visit different parts of the neighborhood. Although there may be trends to these movements, the sampling duration may need to be months to accurately pinpoint "affected" regions. The quantity of data to be analyzed is considerable. Some may need to be stored and reviewed later by the big data analysis engines that are predicting trends based on past history.

Over time, it is noted that this "small" data pattern repeats itself around dusk most nights. "Big" data engines may then infer that a nocturnal animal (e.g., a cat) is causing a "disturbance" in the "reference" signal. Individual chirps and even the combination of chirp streams that create "small" data are unintelligible in isolation. But they may be processed into a more coherent form, which in turn is used to draw conclusions about the environment *not transmitted per se* in each "small" data transmission.

Putting small events together to infer a complex event or trend is difficult, whether in the natural world or the Internet of Things. It may require a control system component, Bayesian reasoning, to filter out the noise from reference signal disruption. "Small" data events, based on observation, propagate "up" for "big" data analysis and action. An immense number of small events feed myriad chirps that may be integrated into complex event analysis.

This example has described only one sort of event (birdsong) in one neighborhood. But as seen in the following section, additional richness in analysis comes when integrator nodes expand on the concept of neighborhoods by actively seeking out and incorporating affinities.

Neighborhoods and Affinities

Internet of Things neighborhoods may be thought of as interesting aggregations of data sources that may be examined and collected by an integrator function. Locating and subscribing to a particular chirp stream may be directed by human programming (e.g., "monitor all moisture sensors in agricultural fields in these four counties").

In this case, the neighborhood is defined geographically, so the integrator function may seek out interesting data streams from many candidates by searching for a particular "signature" of device type (from markers in the chirp packet; see Chapter 6) and location information appended by propagator nodes. Subscribing to these streams allows the integrator function to build up not only a snapshot of current conditions but also to observe changes over time. This data may then be used to generate reports or alarms as needed for human observation.

But the preceding example is not much different from a point-to-point IP data stream type of relationship. In fact, IoT neighborhoods *need not* be bounded by geography, end device type, or any other characteristic. Nor need they be preset by human operators. Instead, they may collect chirps across a wide spectrum of small data flows.

By subscribing to soil moisture sensors, temperature gauges, weather reports, reservoir levels, electric utility time-of-day rates, video images of crop height and ripeness, and so on, it might be possible to create a model that will allow the most cost-effective and timely irrigation of fields, for example. This could be effected either by outputting a report to a human field hand, or the integrator function might simply open the correct valves for the precise time needed (see Figure 2-8).

Independent but *interacting* elements of the real world, each of which is represented by data flows and sources (whether from Internet of Things end devices, the global Internet, or another source) represent affinities of data. These discovered affinities of data may prove to be much more powerful than human programmers might predict in advance. For that reason, it is fundamental that the underlying architecture of the IoT integrator function software allows for independent searching out of potentially interesting data sources by intelligence operating within the integrator functions. (The mechanics of this affinity-seeking intelligence is more fully explored in Chapter 6.)

Note that not every deployed integrator function will incorporate this independent data-seeking capability. In many cases, the role of the integrator function will be more narrowly defined to a specific application or locale, partly for cost and control factors, but also to allow the use of cheaper computing platforms (owing to the need to analyze less data).

Public, Private, and Some of Each

The broad architectural definition of the integrator function and its varied application uses mean that there will be different kinds of neighborhoods formed. This is enabled by the incorporation of public and private markers in the structure of the chirps themselves (see Chapter 6). As in the previous birdsong example, the chirp structure contains both addressing and payload information in a form that will be unintelligible without the proper "key."

Somewhat akin to a Virtual Private Network (VPN) in traditional IP networking, chirps with private markers may traverse a broad network alongside chirps with public markers. In the integrator function publish/subscribe model, security is provided at the end point only. As in trees, where a particular pollen particle may be propagated in any direction, but only a receiver (the flower) programmed to "receive" the message will act upon it, so chirps with a private marker will be inert to any but the desired integrator function.

These private chirps might be seen in Original Equipment Manufacturer (OEM) environments, in which, for example, an application that monitors diesel generators and schedules maintenance as required (low fuel, hot bearing, clogged filter, etc.) might be offered for a specific manufacturer and then only for those units under warranty.

Other chirps (likely the statistical majority) will be public, available for inspection by any "interested" integrator function that builds the chirp stream into a neighborhood. As with emerging social networking norms, in which a wide variety of information is made publicly available by individuals, it is likely that some entities deploying some types of end devices will use public markers only, making those chirp streams available to any integrator function that detects it and subscribes. Again, subscription is an activity of the integrator function only; not of the end device.

It is likely that the some of the most interesting and powerful big data applications of the Internet of Things will come through some combination of public and private chirp streams and small data flows (see Figure 5-6). So hybrid environments with private and public chirp streams sharing portions of propagator networks will be quite common.

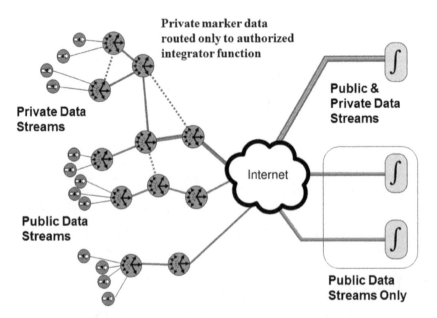

Figure 5-6. Although some proprietary applications will use private markers to restrict use of chirp data, most chirp streams will be fully public for analysis by any "interested" integrator function

Bias Bonus

The potential power of noncontiguous information neighborhoods formed though integrator node affinities selecting among millions of chirp streams is enticing. But seeking out specific chirp streams from desired devices in the cacophony of the Internet of Things will also be important. Especially for OEM and proprietary networks that go beyond generic functions, some method of network tuning may be helpful.

As introduced in Chapter 4, one class of propagator nodes will be equipped with an internal publishing agent that is accessible to one or more integrator nodes. These publishing agents may interact with complementary processes in the integrator function to cause the propagator nodes to preferentially forward some types of packets, perform proprietary chirp bundling, spoof repeated chirps (or refrain from spoofing), and perform other roles on behalf of the integrator function.

In this fashion, integrator functions may construct preferred networks, optimize data flows, and seek out specific types and locations of end devices. The publishing agent–integrator function interaction my again be proprietary or more open. The proprietary interaction is relatively straightforward because there is (by definition) an IP-based connection between integrator function and propagator node. This will allow for secure tuning of data flows between propagator node and integrator function, in a manner similar to a *software-defined network*.

But in a pubic (or mixed) environment, the situation is more complex. Because propagator nodes may be servicing multiple chirp streams, bias must be defined in a way that is neither proprietary nor permanent. The effect of an integrator function on such a (non-private) publishing agent will ebb and flow in an organic way. Repeated interactions with a particular integrator function will bias the propagator more heavily in favor of that integrator functions publish/subscribe requests, as seen in Figure 5-7.

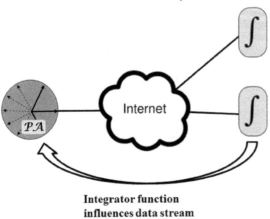

Figure 5-7. *Some classes of propagator nodes will contain publishing agents. The agents interact with integrator functions to "tune" the data forwarding. The bias of the propagator node may be reconfigured over time and fade out if not reinforced by the integrator function. Publishing agents also advertise the availability of potentially interesting new end devices for possible subscription by the associated integrator function*

But if, over time, that interaction ceases or is reduced in frequency, the propagator node will revert to a more promiscuous (nonbiased) forwarding model or will respond to a different integrator function that shows more "interest" by more active biasing. The weights and dwell times of this biasing may be configurable at the propagator node.

Searching for and Managing Agents

Publishing agent–equipped propagator nodes will typically advertise summaries of attached end-device types (including those farther down the "tree" accessed via other propagator nodes), locations, and other characteristics. Integrator functions may use this information to identify publishing agents that have offered interesting chirp streams. (There will also be secure proprietary modes in which propagator nodes do not advertise available data types; instead being specifically targeted by integrator function programming.)

The integrator function establishes a connection to one or (often) many of the publishing agent(s) in order to read and then set certain parameters. It is likely that these publishing-agent-equipped propagator nodes will be placed at logical "junctions" for "branches" of the Internet of Things, creating useful points for management and control. Because publishing agents always reside in propagator nodes that are equipped with an IP gateway, standard IP protocols will be a straightforward medium for their interaction with integrator functions.

This integrator function bias will include settings regarding frequency of transmission for target chirp streams (every chirp, periodic, only when state changes, etc.), exception handling, multicast bundling/pruning, and so on. Propagator nodes will announce discovery of new candidate chirp streams for potential inclusion in preferred forwarding lists. Integrator functions will also restrict the forwarding of some chirp streams to limit the proliferation of unneeded or redundant data.

The biasing of a publishing agent by a particular integrator function is not permanent; over time, requests by other integrator functions may take precedence if there is not "reinforcement" by the originally requesting integrator function. This will allow for organic reconfiguration of the network due to changing needs, seasonality, and other factors.

High- and Low-Level "Loops"

An interesting byproduct of this architecture is that there will essentially be two networking "loops" operating in the network when publishing agents are present in the propagator nodes and are biased by integrator functions.

Propagator-node-based processing for end devices, operating closer to the devices, provides a more equitable distribution of resources. Integrator functions are thus freed from handling communications chores for thousands of end devices.

That more mundane work of pruning and aggregation is then delegated to publish/subscribe agents within the propagator nodes, closer to the end devices. The *control loop* is then effectively split into two isochronous control loops: one loop between the end devices and the biased publish/subscribe agents within propagator nodes, and the second between those agents and their associated subscribing integrator functions.

In the traditional IP-based thin client model, there was effectively one control loop between devices and servers, so end-to-end delays, error checking and correction, and so on are necessary (not to mention a costly full IP stack in each device, as discussed previously). But with the agent located within the propagator node, end devices may continue to converse in simple terse chirps. The end device chirp stream is being converted into a small data flow, to which integrator functions may subscribe. The overall architecture is more scalable and more efficient by *disassociating* the two control loops, as seen in Figure 5-8.

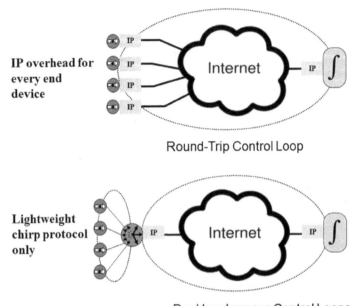

IP overhead for every end device

Round-Trip Control Loop

Lightweight chirp protocol only

Dual Isochronous Control Loops

Figure 5-8. Traditional IP networking models extend the control loop end-to-end, demanding deterministic performance and burdening end devices with expensive processor power and memory. The emerging Internet of Things architecture creates separate control loops, allowing minimal networking investment at the end device and providing better local control without the delays of round-tripping

In this distributed and balanced setting, the publishing agent within the local propagator node acts as an extension of the integrator function, managing the exceptions that interest them: the higher-level loop. The task of pruning and aggregating is delegated to a lower level of control. Round-tripping is obviated.

Using the Mars Rover as an analogy, Mission Control is kept abreast of "interesting" developments, but local control of sensors/actuators is handled autonomously by resident software agents. This obviates needless round-tripping between the rover and earth, providing a more equitable distribution of tasks and resources. This is more efficient because it also reduces both traffic and server load. The output from biased publishing agents is a more palatable edited small data flow.

Regardless of whether device communication is IP- or chirp-based, a layered control loop (with agents as intermediaries acting as the translation mechanisms between the upper and lower control loops) is inherently more efficient than round-tripping.

By contrast, in the traditional IP thin client model, that translation would take place in the cloud, demanding that data originate from end devices in a format palatable to big data consumers. Agents and their location within the lower control loop reduce this burden on the end devices of the IoT.

Agents are bilingual by design. End device-to-publishing agent conversations can be in one language (chirps), more suitable for lower-level conversations. The sensor-motor control loop of the Mars Rover involves a different vocabulary than the command control loop with Mission Control. Local software enables sensors and actuators to be in a close, tight control loop and to do what they were designed for. Other software, with access to this lower control layer, provides Mission Control with the level of granularity needed.

An intermediate agent-based architecture is also closer to the publish/subscribe frameworks that big data systems are familiar with, and so may allow for easy extension to the Internet of Things integrator function architectures. Through web services, cloud servers subscribe to multiple sources of data. Big data systems may be viewed as marketplaces in which publishers/subscribers or data providers and consumers meet and exchange. The "exchange" is one service that enterprise middleware software provides at Layers 7 and above on the network stack. For example, Tibco (www.tibco.com) provides a platform in which real-time feeds are both published and consumed. Multiple and diverse applications employ generic and extensible real-time publish/subscribe "exchange" infrastructure to conduct business. The existence of these models should make the incorporation of integrator function data very straightforward.

Human Interface and Control Points

In the Internet of Things, the integrator function collects the small data flows that develop from combining chirp streams. Somewhat like the human observer in the earlier birdsong example, the integrator function may correlate events and observe patterns from millions of chirps that would be unintelligible (individually or en masse) to a human observer.

Thus the integrator function is the point at which data may be turned into information for consumption by humans. Reports may be generated which highlight conditions in the field, thresholds for certain events calculated and alarms posted, and so on.

For example, a power plant (see Figure 5-9) might monitor thousands of points for temperature variation, vibration, fluid leakage, and other factors. An integrator function would not only monitor individual sensors for out-of-tolerance values but might also examine the interaction of changing values across multiple types of sensors deployed on a variety of equipment. Does an increase in temperature and vibration at a number of related locations represent a potential trouble spot developing, even if no individual sensor is reporting an out-of-tolerance situation? The integrator function could report this situation (and even schedule preventative maintenance), avoiding unexpected downtime under future peak loads.

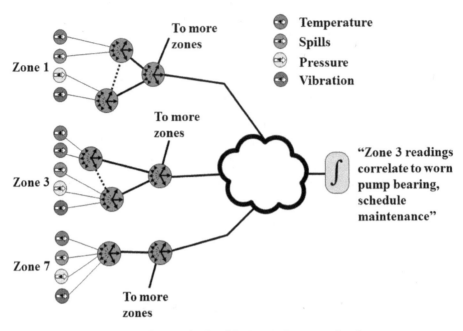

Figure 5-9. *By monitoring thousands of end devices and sensors of various types, an integrator function might infer an impending need for maintenance in a location even though no individual sensor is yet out-of-threshold*

In a complementary way, desired end point settings and configurations may be entered into the integrator function for dissemination across the network. In this case, the integrator function may be given broad commands ("reduce discretionary electrical use"), which results in a wide variety of different end devices at many locations being targets, perhaps in a specific order. In this example, the integrator function might use time-of-day, weather, and other information to determine where and by how much the usage may be cut, rolling the reconfigurations and shutdowns across the globe with regard to the impact of sunlight.

As the name implies, a key characteristic of the integrator function is the intelligent digestion and consolidation of information. For humans interacting with the Internet of Things, the contrasting information of underlying trends and emergent events and alarms are the most important outputs of the integrator function, harnessing the power of myriad IoT end devices.

Machines and Metcalfe

But beyond human interfaces, the IoT integrator function may play a powerful role in pure machine-to-machine networks. In accordance with Metcalfe's Law, the "value" of a communicating network increases with the square of the number of participant members. With large numbers of integrator functions communicating and coordinating with one another, information, resources, and schedules may be shared and optimized without human intervention.

As an example, neighborhood electrical generators plugged into a smart grid energy network with solar panels or wind power sources might be used to support excessive loads during peak times for home appliances. The integrator functions interacting with the various electrical generators and appliances may exchange information to conserve the joint resources and exploit the cheapest sources by studying the patterns in terms of when devices are in use and how much power is typically drawn. The distributed system can thus "schedule" operation into optimal timeslots using Bayesian reasoning.

Over time, machine learning agents within integrator functions may suggest that some competencies be "fused." Fused competencies are, as the name suggests, tightly coupled, largely self-sufficient capabilities between neighborhoods of end devices monitored and controlled by interacting integrator functions.

"Socially networked" integrator functions will also obviously have much broader potential views of events and trends, making possible more useful analysis than any single integrator function.

Collaborative Scheduling Tools

One potentially compelling area for the use of machine-to-machine integrator function interactions is in the area of collaborative scheduling. The example described previously is one instantiation, but broader scheduling efficiencies can be imagined across much broader domains.

The underlying fundamental scheduling principle to be exploited is "cluster" versus "avoid": that is, what activities, events, or elements create more efficiencies when brought together (multiple packages for adjacent addresses sharing the same delivery van, for example) versus those that create more efficiencies when separated (many delivery trucks that must share the same loading dock, for example). By considering a variety of data sources and providing "back pressure" to reschedule or reorder some events or tasks, interacting integrator nodes might allow better use of scarce resources with learning and improved optimization taking place over time.

Packaging and Provisioning

As noted in the introduction, the Internet of Things integrator function is software running on a general-purpose processor with the appropriate performance characteristics and interfaces. With the promulgation of minimal necessary standards and open source code, a wide variety of different organizations and individuals could begin to rapidly create integrator function software to run on many different platforms.

These applications will be programming-intensive to tailor to specific needs, but making available open-source software modules delivering basic functionality will speed deployment. These open-source components are an important part of the Internet of Things development blueprint (see Chapter 8). The possibility of running integrator function software on virtually any device from a smartphone on up permits the analysis and control functionality to scale to any size with off-the-shelf hardware.

Distributed Integrator Functions

To this point, the discussion of integrator functions has assumed a processor location likely some distance (physically and or logically) from the end devices with which it is interacting. And for a significant portion of the Internet of Things, this will likely make sense. As noted elsewhere, for the typical case, data rates will be low, the delivery of any single individual chirp uncritical, and synchronization unimportant. But this will not true everywhere.

Video surveillance and monitoring is one application in which the blasé passenger's description of a bumpy flight is apt: "hours of tedium punctuated by moments of terror." The vast majority of many video surveillance streams are unchanging: the view of a hallway or an unopened gate, perhaps. But the amount of streaming data created by that unchanging scene is substantial, depending on the video CODEC in use.

If all that video data were to be propagated through the Internet to a distant integrator function, the bandwidth, delay, and jitter (variation in delay) would be substantial. But if instead a distributed integrator function were placed at the location of the video camera, substantial processing could be done locally, with only exceptions or events (a human crossing the field of view, for example) generating a message to a distant site and triggering real-time video streaming or recording.

Similarly, process control and other real-time functions might best be served by a localized integrator function that could interpret local conditions from chirps produced by temperature and flow sensors, and then generate chirps to adjust a valve accordingly, as seen in Figure 5-10.

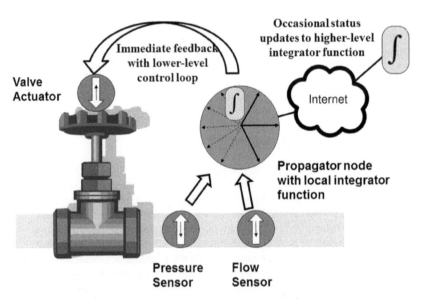

Figure 5-10. *To maximize the response to changing conditions, local flow analysis might take place at an integrator function co-deployed with the nearest propagator. Nominal variations in flow or pressure could be managed by the local action of adjusting valves, whereas periodic status reports and exceptions beyond specific tolerances would be forwarded to an integrator function with a "broader" view*

At the very edges of the Internet of Things, the need for compact integrator function implementations that use a minimum of power and space will demand very small-footprint System-on-a-Chip (SoC) solutions such as Intel's Quark family. These compact microprocessor systems still run standard operating system software and will thus be good targets for rapid development and deployment of distributed integrator function designs, as opposed to fully custom hardware.

In addition to the typical general-purpose processor used for most integrator functions, some distributed integrator functions will certainly also be implemented on customized hardware, often packaged in combination with end device or propagator node hardware.

Location, Location, Location

Application designers determining the optimal location for the IoT integrator function will wish to balance the efficiency of a position near the monitored or controlled devices with the broader perspective that can be gained from placement farther (logically) from the end device. The ability to build a publish/subscribe neighborhood that incorporates varied data sources may outweigh the nominal efficiency of being near the point of analysis or control.

A related decision point is setting the threshold for "phoning home" to a headquarters or oversight location versus managing as best as possible with the information available locally. The incredible diversity of Internet of Things applications will likely create a commensurate variety of deployment approaches.

Filtering the Streams

To make software development and application proliferation easy, the integrator function is specifically architected to operate on general-purpose hardware. Although this type of equipment is well-suited to crunching the large amounts of data potentially generated by thousands or millions of IoT devices, it is generally not optimized for interface to the Internet. Millions of data streams, many of which are of no interest or even ill-intentioned, may arrive at an exposed PC or server Ethernet interface.

In busy applications, handling all this traffic to search out the meaningful IoT small data streams would slow the main processor and reduce its capacity for the main integrator function tasks. So the emerging Internet of Things architecture allows for an additional appliance called the *filter gateway*.

The filter gateway sits between the global Internet and the general-purpose processor (see Figure 5-11). Essentially its function is as a "two-armed" router (for example, Gigabit Ethernet in/Gigabit Ethernet out), providing network service, security, and firewall capabilities. The filter gateway simply discards non-relevant data to reduce the load on the general-purpose hardware running the integrator function software.

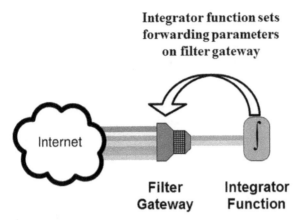

Integrator function sets
forwarding parameters
on filter gateway

Internet

Filter   Integrator
Gateway   Function

Figure 5-11. Filter gateways act as firewalls to off-load network interface tasks from the general-purpose processors running integrator function software

It is likely that existing router and/or security appliance hardware may be adapted to this role. A key software addition to off-the-shelf or open-source devices will be a publishing agent within the filter gateway. It will perform the same function as the publishing agent found in some classes of propagator nodes, allowing the integrator function to "tune" the data streams it sends and receives through the biasing techniques described previously.

Accessing the Power of the Internet of Things

The integrator function turns the numberless streams of data from Internet of Things end devices into rich publish/subscribe information sources and extracts meaning from potential chaos. In the next chapter, the protocols of the emerging Internet of Things architecture are explored in detail.

CHAPTER 6

■ ■ ■

Architecture for the Frontier

The general architecture of the Internet of Things (IoT) has been introduced in the preceding chapters, including concepts such as terse self-classified chirp protocols, structured tree networks, and the publish/subscribe framework. In addition, there has been an introduction to the key building blocks of the emerging Internet of Things: end devices, propagator nodes (and associated publishing agents), and integrator functions (and associated filter gateways). This chapter will explore the deeper architectural details of the Internet of Things, beginning with chirp formation at the edge of the network and continuing through to the propagation though the network, and finally to the implications of a publish/subscribe IoT world.

The key principle of the Internet of Things architecture is the segregation of networking cost and complexity to the propagator nodes, permitting much simpler components and architectures at the billions of simple end devices. These intermediate elements then bridge the gap between raw data chirps and big data meaning. With the assumption that the networking capabilities are in place within propagator nodes, individual end device appliances, sensors, and actuators may be implemented with a simple specialized language and vocabulary: the bare minimum necessary for what they were designed to do. Each type of device can use its own specialized format to chirp in its own dialect—no overarching standard common language is needed in every end device. Devices can remain simple, whereas propagator nodes (and publishing agents, if installed) can be arbitrarily complex.

A Necessary Alternative to IP

Beyond efficiency (large packet formats, etc.), there is a more fundamental reason to support a different transport protocol instead of couching a new description language inside the payload section of an IP packet. And the key factor is the need to support a one-to-many/many-to-one publish/subscribe framework.

Recall that the packet type ID in the IP packet header provides the information needed to drive traditional IP routing according to associated packet handlers. Adding a large number of new packet handlers, vocabulary, and protocols optimized to support the exploding variety of Internet of Things end devices to IP would pose challenges of scale, scope, and manageability. Routers would need software revisions to know how to route these new types of packets. That new software would in turn need to be deployed across the entire router network core and edge routers, including hundreds of thousands of legacy routers.

IP formats were originally designed for only the coarsest classifications of packet-type routing handlers; for example, voice, video, web browsing, and file transfer. Application-specific granularity (such as Devices ➤ Sensors ➤ Moisture ➤ Device-Type-A) cannot be easily expressed in a traditional format that was intended to address sender-oriented communications based on IP addresses and MAC IDs. If this type of data granularity were to be expressed within the payload section of an IP packet, the process of peering deep into each payload would slow down traffic unacceptably at each network device. These are the inherent limitations to IP sender-oriented, point-to-point traffic flow.

A Big Problem, and Getting Bigger

Although there are many expected classifications for appliance, sensor, and actuator types, this will be an evolving field into perpetuity. Providing specialized packet handlers within traditional IP routers to handle the routing needs of end device types yet undreamed-of is simply not practical. New types of end devices—and combinations of end devices, as illustrated in Figure 6-1—will constantly be added to the Internet of Things. There will also be the need for real-time localized control of semiautonomous relationships between sensors and actuators (see Figure 6-2), creating localized communities of machine-to-machine communications that are just beginning.

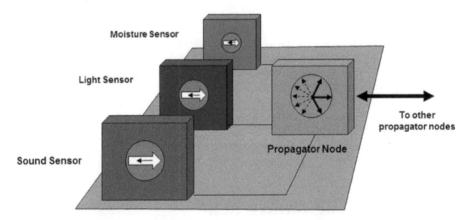

Figure 6-1. Combinations of different sensor types within one physical package, each generating uniquely marked chirp packets, are just one example of the benefits of self-classified chirp protocols. In this example, an on-board propagator node could efficiently combine the chirp streams into "busloads" of small data for interpretation by one or more integrator functions

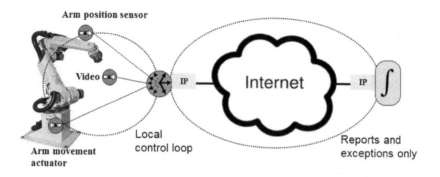

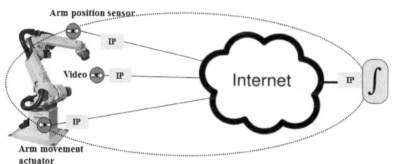

Figure 6-2. *In many emerging applications, local feedback from sensors and the corresponding commands to actuators will be needed in real time. A local control loop, illustrated here, uses data from positioning and video sensors to guide actuator movements (top). The risks, costs, and time associated with sending the real-time control traffic round-trip to a server(bottom) is not viable due to the risks of delay, jitter, and/or lost control packets (whether chirp-based or IP). But status reports and exceptions may still be reported to higher-level integrator functions while the local control loop manages real-time needs*

These new applications will thus require their own private small data streams and/or terse, tight local control loops. Standards-committee processes for IP and backbone routing take a long time and are understandably biased toward maintaining the status quo: that is, IP protocols used for nearly all communications (including the Internet of Things). Despite this, a more organic underlying architecture is needed that can be adapted rapidly to new end devices, independent of the techniques used for data transmission and analysis.

The primary reason for chirp–based end devices is their inherent simplicity and the fact that the chirp protocol may organically evolve to support device categories not yet dreamed of, let alone yet defined as to how they interact with humans and the world. Burdening these emerging publisher/subscriber relationships with the detritus and restrictions of a solely IP-based transport scheme is simply too small a canvas for the developers of these new products to create within (or to manage, build, and afford to produce once designed).

An Alternative Inspired by Nature

To solve problems of massive scale and generic broadcast infrastructures, nature uses a *receiver-oriented architecture*. Pollen "publishers" (plants) have no "receiver" (flower) address per se, nor do they know where their ultimate destination will be. A pollen category–based identification scheme is receiver-oriented: the self-categorized pollen simply travels in all possible directions; it is not destination-based or flowing in a predefined point-to-point relationship. It is the onus of the subscriber to accept (target flower) or reject (sneezing allergic human) the pollen. Publishing within classified categories in a natural environment (defined by genus and species) connects pollen to flowers in an inherently more efficient manner, but nature allows for evolution to take place over time. Thus, the "protocol" of pollen is externally marked with a self-classification recognized by receivers and may change over time.

A Protocol Based on Category Classifications

What would a similar extensible protocol look like within the chirp structures of the Internet of Things? In nature's DNA sequencing, there are strands of genetic code that are recognizable. Sometimes these specific genetic sequences serve as a marker that helps identify a distinct DNA sequence: relationships can be seen as the sequences repeat. Genetic fingerprinting is extensible as scientists learn more and more and can probe deeper into smaller sequences of information. The markers point to meaningful locations within the DNA sequence.

In nature's world of publish/subscribe, pollen is being published for subscriber flowers. Pollination is essentially a selective pattern match. The same logic will be applied to the IoT publish/subscribe world. In this case, rather than the wind distributing pollen promiscuously, a network of propagator nodes may use the structure of the chirp packet to direct data to an appropriate "receiver."

Chirp packets intentionally lack a target address; in a publish/subscribe world, the *receiver* chooses chirp streams and small data flows. So when these chirps are received by the first propagator node, what is needed to forward the arriving chirps in the appropriate direction? Recall that propagator nodes are aggregating and pruning chirps to form multichirp packets for transmission to the appropriate adjacent propagator node for eventual delivery to the integrator function(s).

Skeletal Architecture of Chirp Packets

A system that locates the end device publishers and integrator function subscribers efficiently and develops the correct routes is of common interest to both publishers and subscribers. Propagator nodes, as discussed previously, require some category description from the end devices to enable the matchmaking. What does this descriptor look like?

As an analogy, consider again bird chirps, the sounds of which may be organized based on the study of individual bird categories. Bird types may be identified by chirp/tune/melody. Hence those subscribers interested in melodies from doves can now receive those recordings, based on a bird category. The categories will have to support different levels of granularity—some bird enthusiasts are interested only in doves near their homes. Hence the category field should be sufficiently flexible in design to support further drill-down.

In nature, melody/tunes and DNA structures incorporate marker strands of information that provide a common pattern across members of the category. The same is true for markers within Internet of Things chirp packets. These markers occur at specific locations and are of specific defined patterns.

A familiar example is the global telephone numbering system, in which information of increasing granularity is found in known standard locations. Country code, area code, exchange, and subscriber identification are progressively used to route the call to its final destination.

Within the Internet of Things, the final destination may not be known (again, due to the publish/subscribe nature of the IoT). So the chirps must be self-classified in a similar granular fashion to allow other network elements to act upon them.

For example, a given chirp category may have an 8-bit marker, which is always found in the fourth byte of the bit stream. (This pattern is indicated by the format of the chirp packet's offset marker, as shown in Figure 6-3).

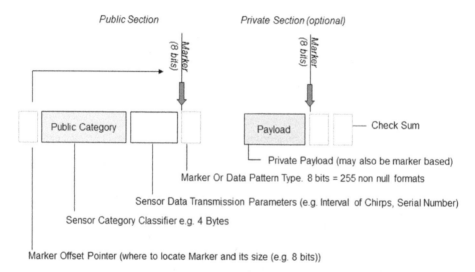

Figure 6-3. *The marker offset pointer allows IoT elements to recognize the locations of the chirp packet's public and private markers without examining more deeply within the packet, making routing and other networking decisions more rapid. The markers in turn provide information on how to interpret the end device's self-classified category and type*

One way of expressing this category classification is seen through an example. Consider a combination of a 4-byte classification and one additional marker byte of 8 bits. This can be expressed as 4.8(*XXXX*), where *XXXX* are more levels of granularity that may be gleaned from the 4 bytes by knowing the specific marker pattern format of the 8 bits and what that format entails. In this case, the 8-bit marker explains how to decode the 4-byte public classification. This will include the end device type (moisture sensor versus street light, for example) and the way the 4 bytes of data are structured. The 4.8 pattern format alone would be sufficient information for a propagator node to make basic routing decisions (see below).

Additional information can be obtained from the value of the 8-bit marker. Consider an 8-bit marker pattern that is 1.1.1.1.1.1.1.1 (or 255). This value of 255 may indicate a format in which each of the preceding 4 bytes is a 1-byte classification subcategory. Thus, a 4-byte category may now be interpreted as A.B.C.D., where the letters occupy 1 byte each and indicate some subcategory. The complete interpretation of the category is thus 4.8.255.A.B.C.D.

The chirp packet will also contain the actual payload of the sensor values, but note that these have not been discussed so far. This is intentional, as it demonstrates that the propagator node may route quickly and efficiently on only the first bytes of data received without deeper examination of the chirp packet.

This enables a quick bit mask to look for all publishers in categories 4.8.255, and so on. Propagator nodes with internal publishing agents capable of acting upon further granularity in the chirp signature will need to access a reference that provides a map or implicit field markers for A.B.C.D within the category field. Thus, it can be imagined that all of the following provide successively deeper classifications of the chirp packet:

4.

4.8.

4.8.255

4.8.255.A

4.8.255.A.B

Thus, the propagator nodes, depending on their access to internal field data, can provide multiple levels of granularity in addressing (and may potentially act upon the complete chirp packet through a publishing agent that is aware of the meaning of the full address).

The simplest category of 4.8 may be sufficient for coarse aggregation: chirps of the same "feather" may be flocked together (see the "Scheduling the Bus" section that below). But additional levels of granularity in propagator node bus scheduling and routing are supported by considering more data.

Larger and infrequent buses might cover 4.8.XX categories, while smaller "shuttles" for more-frequently-requested data may specify precisely what is of interest; e.g., 4.8.255.A.B.C.XX. Chirp self-categorization thus drives the loading of multichirp–packet forwarding buses, their contents, and their frequency, at differing levels of granularity.

Note that A.B.C.D is distinct from B.A.C.D. In general, there are 4*4*4*4 or 255 non-null combinations for a four-letter vocabulary: A, B, C, D.

Obviously, the 255 combinations allowed provide tremendous flexibility in the way the 4-byte category is interpreted. Like DNA, the alphabet may be terse and small, but the patterns depicting the categories are not. An exceptional variety of content may thus be expressed within short chirp packets.

In fact, the category system is flexible enough that the simplest data payloads may be expressed within the public category *alone* with no separate payload. They would be very basic states expressible in a few bytes.

Individual Information within Chirp Signatures

Beyond category information, bird chirps also carry individual and private information. Nature's random number generator changes the individual birds chirp tonal qualities governing each bird. This serves as a form of identification. Thus, mother birds know each of their children's distinctive chirps, although all are using the same broad general chirp format and its associated shared vocabulary.

The Internet of Things counterpart of this sort of individual identification within the chirp packet is labeled "Sensor Data Transmission Parameters" in Figure 6-3. In combination with the "Sensory Category Classifier" seen in Figure 6-3, chirp identification parameters can include the following:

- Chirps with distinctively different patterns (i.e., tunes)

- Public category classification, including some specific (though not unique) end device identification; e.g., the last four digits of the manufacturer stock keeping unit (SKU) number of the device

Additional identification information is added by the connecting propagator node:

- **Lineage based:** For example, an end device associated with a kitchen propagator node

- **Location based:** For example, located in a kitchen, close to the toaster (derived from signal strength analysis, not a logical connection)

Note that the combination of a chirp tune (in this example, its last 4 SKU digits), its location, and its lineage *collectively* can define a distinct end device sensor or actuator. Although none is globally unique, the *combination* will likely be sufficiently distinctive for the vast majority of applications. The absolute uniqueness of the address *is not* required.

The combinations have inherent randomness because their constituent elements (e.g. transmission pattern of chirps) are random. They are not required to be unique, as are IP or MAC ID addresses, so there is no burden of maintaining a global database. Purely local "pretty good" distinction in the bird chirp is sufficient for the mother bird. By the same token, "pretty good" distinction for local end devices is sufficient for propagator nodes.

Note that individual data, while often in the private section, may also be present in the public section. Thus, some common types of end devices (e.g., temperature sensors) may not need a private section: the data may not need to be secured.

"Light" Error Detection and Security

The combination of marker and public category classification provides a first level of light error detection. For example, if the 8-bit marker described previously calls for a 4-byte category classification, but some other value is found instead, an error is recognized, and the chirp is discarded. Similarly, if the marker is corrupted and does not match the (correct) category classification, the chirp is likewise discarded. This is the reason why the marker occurs after the category classification within the chirp packet; it acts as a simple error-detection mechanism without creating any additional overhead.

Errors that occur elsewhere deeper in the chirp packet may elude this first level of error-checking, but any mismatches of markers and classification will eventually be detected. The presence of any propagator node that compares the sequences within the chirp stream will eventually result in this chirp being discarded. Because chirps are typically repetitive, the loss of this single corrupted chirp is not critical. Note, however, that corrupted chirps are being progressively pruned; often *before* the chirps are combined into IP packets.

Unlike the capabilities of IP packet headers, this light error detection allows a small number of errors to be propagated through part of the local network. But the savings in overhead for each chirp packet is well worth the small cost of handling some bad packets through portions of the network.

Generic Chirp Handling

The deeper chirp packet examination described above pertains primarily to propagator node networks containing publish/subscribe agents. If the propagator node has no publishing agent installed, small data flows are managed by the network topology and the arrow of transmission incorporated in the public marker: either toward integrator functions or toward end devices.

Here, the network topology of uplinks and downlinks (refer to Chapter 4) is being used to help move data toward an appropriate destination. Note that the directions can encompass both the propagator node topology and the parent IP–based network tree in a hybrid mesh network that incorporates both.

Incognito Chirp Transport

Some classification categories of chirps might have to travel incognito. That is, they expect propagators to rebroadcast them, potentially in all directions, until an appropriate publishing agent or integrator function discovers them.

"Incognito" chirp streams create the equivalent of a Virtual Private Network (VPN) within the IoT. They constitute a category that is indecipherable by nonproprietary publishing agents and integrator functions. Although they may be transported generically by the propagator node network, they typically could not pass through the chirp-to-IP interface as is. In the typical application, there will be a separate propagator node with a corresponding proprietary publishing agent somewhere on the "chirp" side of the network that has the "key" to interpret the private information within the chirp packets. From this, they may generate IP traffic that could traverse the global Internet to be acted upon by integrator functions also programmed to be part of the incognito network.

A "4.0" category chirp implies a marker at byte 4, but its length is not specified. Agents with bit mask filtering can locate such semi-incognito chirps because they know what the marker is. Note that the marker can be arbitrarily long or short. Short markers increase the occurrence of false positives with other marker types (e.g., the 4-bit marker 1.0.1.1 shares 4 bits with the 8-bit marker 1.0.1.1.0.0.1.1). Publishing agents that have this level of information can also glean other data from the packet melody/strands to filter out undesired or malformed chirp packets; these packets will not cross over to the IP network.

A "0.0" category chirp does not specify either the location or size of the marker. This is *completely* incognito, and the propagator node may continue to rebroadcast the chirp both up and down the propagator node tree until it reaches end devices, a publishing agent within a propagator node, or integrator functions of the network (depending on the arrow of transmission). Recall that native chirp devices have no access to the IP network except through propagator nodes, so IP traffic congestion is limited.

In some situations, a 0.0 chirp might want to specify the arrow of transmission and nothing else (e.g., up or down the tree). Because each category has its own vocabulary and language, privately defined 0.0 chirp families may choose to use a unique location in the chirp packet for the arrow of transmission. Languages defining the meaning of the data comprised of bit streams are both versatile and secure because they are generally receiver-oriented and do not require a deeper understanding within the propagator nodes.

IP-based end devices may also use category patterns as part of their data classification schemes. In that case, IP-based packet headers will specify the end device MAC ID or serial number within the payload along with the category classification. IP-based agents in the integrator functions or local to the IP interface of a publishing agent–equipped propagator node could then act on end device identification and category classification. Thus, a single integrator function may incorporate chirp streams aggregated into small data flows transmitted over IP and the traditional Internet, as well as more sophisticated end devices sending and receiving in native IP.

By the same token, end devices may include a specific IP address where they want their chirps to be sent in their private payload or public category type. The chirp interface of a publishing agent–equipped propagator node receives this chirp, which may be pruned and repackaged as needed for IP transmission to the specified address.

Transmission Agility Information within the Chirp

If chirping end devices share the same wireless medium (such as in Wi-Fi), one part of the public category section will also contain chirp transmission characteristics. In other words, the basic chirp structure must support network agility, even if a large majority of the end devices cannot act upon it *themselves*. Smarter, more agile devices can become aware that simpler chirp devices will be active at the intervals specified.

Thus, data related to when and how often the end devices chirp and what pattern they use (as in melody/tunes or rhythm) is needed by both propagator nodes and smarter agile end devices to ensure that elements of the network can anticipate and hear chirps distinctly and without collocated interference on the same "channel" from other devices. (Note that in nature, bird chirps are often interleaved; birds are aware of each other and may actively avoid transmitting simultaneously.)

This data also gives propagator nodes the option to shift smarter, more agile chirp devices to other times. Or the propagator node, after review of local client device transmission patterns, can forward a request for a change to the dipswitch settings of a simple end device. An indication of whether specific end devices support such flexibility is again part of the pattern marker. Thus, after some tuning, there may be sufficient distinction in the melodies so that propagator nodes can easily recognize individual end device "offspring" by their pattern of transmission.

Extensible, Nonunique, Pattern-driven

A broader view of the chirp architecture emerges. It contains patterns, defining other patterns, each of which provides a more refined level of detail. Defined levels of access to that detail can reveal:

- What type (category)of chirp is being transported?

- How often is this data published?

- What is its publishing frequency pattern? (Perhaps it is dynamic or it may need observation over time, implying learning and discovery.)

- What are the distinguishing features of individual chirp devices, such as serial number, location, and lineage?

- What is the information on the transmission pattern that enables agile devices to share the same medium without interference?

Note that all of this information is easily discerned by rudimentary bit masks—that is, *if* a particular pattern is known. One example is a propagator node that is instructed to look at bit location 13 in all 4.8.11 packets. If that bit is set to "1", it indicates a universal flag for "unit malfunction, type 1". The propagator node is required to convert that information into an IP packet and forward it to the manufacturer specified in another segment of the chirp packet.

The public section defines the chirp category needed for bus scheduling and packaging of packets (as noted previously). Without this category information, the propagator node would not know which direction to send the packets, as in which bus route to employ going up or down trees, and where to clone more packets for multicast transmissions when multiple subscribers exist.

The second, often private, section is the message: what a particular end device is saying and some (typically proprietary) information about this end device. It uses the same concepts as the public section, but it has its own markers and definitions of what those patterns signify and hence the location the implicit private field markers. The 4.8.11.A.B.C.D category family may use a completely different scheme for the *private* section than the 4.8.11.A.B.D.C category family.

The public and private parts of the chirp packet are separated by a publically known *public section end marker* that can be of variable lengths. For example, it may be 4 bits or 8, depending when whether 15 or 255 different types of (public) chirp patterns are needed.

Some default public markers will be provided through consensus or standards bodies and working groups (see Chapter 8). They will be reserved for common use by end device manufacturers of a specific category (e.g., all moisture sensor manufacturers might use a category such as A.B.C.D.E.F, a 6-byte category address).

Category Byte Size

Many simple devices may require only 1 byte for a category (255 variants) and another 4-bit marker for the pattern type (see Figure 6-4). Thus, each of the 255 category numbers may be interpreted up to 15 distinct ways. This allows for close to 212 interpretations of a

1-byte category field. Similarly, a 6-byte category field would allow for (248 -1) variants, each supporting 255 patterns (8-bit marker). The "genetic code" describing an end device category may be expressed in multiple ways using this extensible pattern based-format, which would permit additional categories to be defined over time.

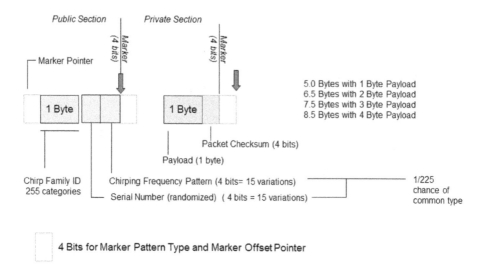

Figure 6-4. *Chirp packet size is variable; appliances, sensors, and actuators sending or receiving only small amounts of data may have a correspondingly low overhead applied to their chirp packets. Markers indicating chirp packet length are external to the data field to allow quick analysis by network elements and incorporate device type and classification*

For non-incognito (non-zero-byte) public sections, the marker type provides all the information needed to interpret it. The pattern defines where the content subsections/fields reside within the public section. Hence simple devices may use a larger public section to include data that is *also public*. Here, no private section is needed or used.

A zero-byte location is defined to mean that there is no public section. The marker type points to a data pattern that provides the information needed to interpret the private section, following the (empty) public section. The marker pattern is then used to interpret what follows generally as a payload. Thus, the flexible use of the marker pattern is supported beyond its initial intended use. A marker pattern and the associated classification of the data packet may together constitute an IP packet payload. This is relevant to IP-based sensor streams that prefer native IP connectivity over chirp-to-IP bridging through propagator nodes.

Marker Pattern Templates

Sharing the same marker type at the specified locations within the chirp packet engenders collaboration between manufacturers of the same sensor type. They may agree to jointly use a range of marker types (200–220, for example), which would be common fields, but each may then use other fields (both in the public and private sections) to provide more detailed and/or secure information. A shared used marker pattern template emerges through this collaboration.

Creating a new marker type (say, 221) may not require the traditional central standards body review process because the repercussions are limited to that group of manufacturers. For example, introducing a new marker type in location 1, affects only the 1-byte public category users. Within that, it affects those who want to use the same marker pattern number. Contrast this with the challenges inherent in defining a new IP header format. IP headers must universally comply with IP requirements in order to be readable, with any change potentially affecting all users.

The marker template is therefore an organically evolving pattern-masking scheme that helps integrator functions delve deeper into the public section/category classification ID. As such, it loosely resembles IPv4 or IPv6, which are subsections of the entire IP address.

Note, however, that IP addressing is destination-based, so after the packet reaches its destination the payload is extracted. Then the information, perhaps still device-specific, must be device-abstracted. Next come pruning and aggregation in the generation of small data. The small data is now publishable within the distributed processing of big data servers (e.g. Apache Hadoop–based). It must now be inserted into the publish/subscribe framework of web-based services.

The situation is much simpler in the Internet of Things through the use of chirp category marker templates. Small data streams are generated closer to the end device source by propagator nodes, in which data can potentially have more real-time impact in tighter sensing-control-actuation loops. And because chirp-based traffic is category-based, finer granularity is simply a matter of loading the appropriate publishing agents at any level within the propagator node network or chirp-aware integrator functions that know how to look into IP encapsulations of aggregated small data.

The category section is a bit stream with contiguous fields, like strands in a DNA sequence. Knowing how to look into it helps better decipher the end device chirp category. But this requires more processing and is therefore intended for integrator function subscribers interested in finer granularity. As the chirp streams become aggregated into small data flows and move through the network, information continues to be disseminated with finer targeting to the interested integrator function subscribers, who can also drill down, if they prefer, by requesting broader category searches. As noted in Chapter 5, this can be through biasing of the publishing agents within propagator nodes that are so-equipped.

But even without a publishing agent within the propagator nodes, the lowest level of granularity needed is simply the marker location and its number. Hence, a byte 6, 4-bit marker, with value 1.0.1.1 is sufficient to have the chirp aggregated toward an appropriate agent for type 06.4.11. This may be a publishing agent in another propagator node or an integrator function.

Finer Control via Agents

At the first agent with an *understanding* of 6.4 buses, specialized 6.4.11 processes may peruse the category pattern to uncover two more subcategories, each of which might be specified by the pattern description to be 1 byte each. Such an expanded category might be interpreted as 6.4.11.250.250. Subscribers willing to pay for this level of detail are alerted to the availability of a small data stream with that category classification. Thus end-device chirps can be very specific in terms of the type of agent they may be transmitted toward using a variable pattern template structure.

Publishing agents in the propagator node path allow chirp streams of specific types to somewhat manage the network that carries them because manufacturers can decide where those agents are placed along the route, starting with 6.4.11 and becoming progressively finer.

The "bus" transmission schedules of aggregated packets are now driven by the amount of traffic and any delivery timing specifics set by the subscribing integrator function(s). The size and content of the small data streams are being managed to ensure timely delivery in dynamically changing scenarios. This becomes a more tractable problem as more exploration into the chirp category is possible closer to the chirp publishers. However, having pattern matching agents 6.8.001 through 6.8.255 (8-bit marker) resident at a local propagator node requires more CPU processing, which may be suitable for an enterprise application propagator node but it is overkill for the home.

Hence, multiple types of propagator nodes emerge, some perhaps to generate small data streams for specific category types. Or SIM cards slots may be provided, so that additional categories of chirp packet–handling publishing agents may be supported. Some of these bus-handling specializations will be secured to specific hardware; others may be software agents/apps.

Scheduling the Bus

The "bus-loading" process is roughly akin to placing human passengers on the proper bus route to reach the appropriate destination. For schoolchildren on the first day of classes, the available information might be the passenger's name and grade from a nametag. While the child does not know the correct route or even the destination address, the teacher supervising bus loading has the requisite knowledge of the routing network to make correctly decide upon which bus to place the passenger.

At the propagator node, then, arriving chirp packets will be collected and then be directed to the "bus" (transmission path) best suited for them. This must be determined largely by public information provided by the chirp packet markers. (If there are publishing agents deployed within the propagator node network, chirp packets may be examined further to determine how they should be forwarded or discarded.)

Ultimately, only the subscribing receiver, typically an integrator function, will look at the *full* chirp to determine if there is information sought by that receiver. The propagator nodes need only basic information from the chirp packet markers to make initial routing decisions. Further, there can be small changes in the data; it need not be error-free. As long as the markers are not corrupted, the faulty data will still find its way along the network.

Propagators simply need to know what direction to send the data – up or down the network tree in light of the transmission "arrow" found within a marker. This is not complex in a tree structure with $O(n)$ routing (see sidebar "Why Trees Scale" in Chapter 4). Recall, this is not a peer-to-peer network, requiring an $O(n2)$ computation of the routing paths, as suggested by traditional sensor networks, e.g. ZigBee. Thus, the direction (up/down) suffices in tree structures. And the direction for an end device chirp packet should point to where subscribers are.

Routing on Category Classifications

The shared routing table within the meshed propagator node network keeps track of where the clients are, includes chirp devices and publishing agents. Some chirp routing agents may be on the chirp-to-IP bridge, and capable of securely accessing the entire category fingerprint, perusing the contents and decide what to do with it.

The efficient path of the chirp data is thus gated, filtered and then redirected at progressively finer sieves, akin to Zip code classifications for postal mail. Letters that fit "standard" patterns (size and weight) are processed efficiently. Others will be dealt with after the simple stuff is completed—this is how greedy algorithms work. The price paid for the flexible chirp format is that nonstandard package types will emerge and must be handled, albeit less efficiently.

For maximum efficiency in local pruning and aggregation, it is best to place publishing agents closer to the end devices' raw published data streams. Here the publishing agents have more control over what is forwarded and how. A subscription model would defray the cost of transport and pruning.

In addition to the task of aggregation in building small data stream buses, propagator nodes may also be required to perform pruning in response to their subscriber preferences. Traffic flowing upward from remote moisture sensors in the wine country in France to an Amazon-hosted cloud service in the United States could well be small, but given the number of such sensors, the IP traffic is significant. IP traffic is not free; some means to control what is sent over IP is needed—specifically, the pruning of repetitive data close to its source (as opposed to at the integrator function).

As an example, in one network there might be a handful of 4.8.XX chirp category end devices; others are all 2.4.XX or 6.8.XX. It would make sense to move the 4.8.XX agents to a propagator node that handles more 4.8.XX buses. A 4.8.XX bus central "hub" emerges, at least temporarily, based on the center of gravity where 4.8.XX end devices and their subscribers are located. Some chirps may have more hops to travel; but by economies of scale, 4.8.XX bus deliveries and scheduling become easier and less costly.

Dynamic loading on the network is examined by the propagator nodes forming the hybrid mesh tree (of both IP and chirp devices) from the IP connection downward toward the chirp end devices. System administrators are notified as to the best locations to locate publishing agents on the propagator nodes. This will alter the data paths and streamline flow. Further, if the publishing agent is mobile (as in not locked-in to a particular physical device), the network can automatically move the publishing agents to optimize overall traffic flows. This is akin to changing the physical network topology to meet changing latency and throughput requirements.

Managing the Load

Both the physical network topology and the logical network (based on where publishing agents and integrator functions reside) eventually stabilize and learn to adapt the topology to provide stable, tunable bus forwarding schedules and routes for the small data streams.

Chirps may be merged, pruned, or aggregated at each propagator node along the path, based both on network topology and (if present) publishing agent biasing by integrator functions. This is necessary for a variety of reasons: some repetitive data may be discarded, new paths discovered, rerouting around failures and congestion, termination of subscriptions by integrator functions, and so on. The "publish" and "subscribe" sides of the Internet of Things are thus in dynamic alignment.

Propagator Node Networks and Operation

The foregoing chirp architectures and routing algorithms are acted upon by an interconnected network of propagator nodes and the traditional Internet, as introduced in Chapter 4. For the reason outlined there, tree-like structures are chosen as the most scalable and efficiently self-organizing structure for these networking elements of the Internet of Things. The propagator node network connects the end devices at the frontier of the Internet of Things without requiring IP connectivity end to end.

Trees are older than man and have a highly evolved networking structure that is both efficient and adaptive. The structure is recursive: any part of the tree replicates the same structure. The underground roots are an inverted tree and branches are miniature horizontal trees, all connected through the trunk. In a network of trees, some are "rooted" to the tree trunk; others through relay nodes. The logical and physical network of branches all follow one simple rule: the "uplink" (the head of the branch) is always one. A pitch fork branch (one with three roots to the tree trunk) would be considered a freak of nature. It is this simple rule—one uplink only—that ensures O(n) routing. Scalable networks are thus possible.

A Tree Grows in the IoT

Nature's tree structure is emulated in the emerging IoT architecture. For example, consider the propagators P0, P1, P2, and P3, as shown in Figure 6-5. P0 is the "root" node because it has access to the IP network. P0-P1-P2 form a "string of pearls" relay for chirp clients C3 and C4. C3 and C4 both share the lineage P0.P1.P2 and hence are identified as siblings. This lineage becomes part of their identity.

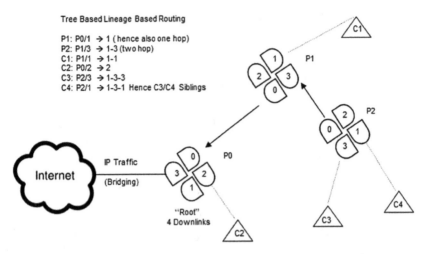

Figure 6-5. *Propagator nodes form a structured tree for networking efficiency. The propagator node with an IP connection (typically to the Internet) is designated as the "root" node. The rest organize their links accordingly, designating links as "uplinks" (toward the IP connection) and "downlinks" (away from the IP connection)*

Propagator nodes form sections of a subtree, the simplest example of which is a string of pearls (e.g., P0 ➤ P1 ➤ P2). Forming a link in the chain requires at least two interfaces: uplink and downlink transceivers. "Transceivers" here may be any form of network link: wired or wireless at a variety of speeds and with a wide variety of protocol types. Each separate transmission path or channel is a networking "slot" that may be assigned as a link in the growing topology. Generally speaking, "uplink" corresponds to moving toward the IP "root"; "downlink" is moving away.

For example, P1 slot 0 is an uplink connecting to P0 Slot 0. P2 slot 3 is a downlink providing connectivity to P2 uplink slot 0. By convention, slot 0 refers to the uplink, except for root nodes (P0). "Root" propagator nodes have only downlinks; their uplink is the IP bridge connecting either to a directly attached integrator function or (more typically) to the global Internet.

The propagator nodes in Figure 6-5 are shown with four transceivers, which could be infrared LEDs or other short-range wireless transceivers. They are placed in the general vicinity and with arbitrary orientation. Propagator nodes periodically scan the environment and reorient/reassign the slots, so there is always one uplink connecting to a parent propagator node. The choice is based on the best available effective throughput, all the way back to a root propagator node.

The parent selections are not always based on the smallest number of "hops" to the Root (a hop is counted for each propagator node in the chain). For example, P2 may be able to "see" P0, but the throughput of the direct link between P0 and P2 is inferior overall to a path from P0to P1and on to P2. In the event it was not, P2 would logically reorient its uplink, so Slot 3 would now be the Uplink facing Slot 0 of P0.

Thus, a -slot propagator node, with arbitrary orientation, may logically reassign slots 0 through 3 to ensure connectivity back to an upstream root node. The slots 0 to 3 are thus being dynamically reassigned to maintain an effective tree-based network topology.

Propagator nodes are placed in locations where they can connect to end devices and form a chain of propagator-node-to propagator-node tree branches as shown previously, all the way back to a "root" node (that bridges to IP). The primary function of the propagator nodes is to send upstream "relevant" data. In some cases, this data is being promiscuously forwarded in a public way, based simply on the arrow of transmission (toward the end device or toward the propagator node).

In other cases, the publishing agents residing within propagator nodes may be biased by integrator functions to include and exclude certain classes and categories of data based on the markers contained within the chirp streams (as described previously).

Choosing Parents Wisely

At the most basic level, propagator nodes are relays. Relays connecting to a "root" node form the branches of a tree. On power up, the primitive behavior is to become associated with a parent that provides a path upstream to the root propagator node. Generally, the closer the parent to the root propagator node, the better. The preference may therefore be, at a rudimentary level, to connect to parents with a low hop count: 0 for the root, 1 for one removed, and so on.

In a general sense, it can be expected that the bulk of Internet of Things traffic is moving mostly toward integrator functions reached via the global Internet, so there is more traffic and contention for bandwidth closer to the root propagator node. Hence, in addition to noting the candidate parent propagator nodes within its connection "zone," propagator nodes must also be able to send a "probe request" to determine the signal quality for transmission. Additionally, each device would need to know how many "sibling" propagator nodes it must contend with for access to the IP root. Siblings are additional propagator nodes linked to the same parent.

Because sibling propagator nodes are part of their own subtrees, the descendants of those siblings are also indirectly competing for the parent node's resources. In short, a tremendous amount of information must be sifted through before a propagator node selects a parent. And the situation can change unpredictably. A simplified notification of the presence to a candidate parent is required. At the base level, connected nodes transmit, through housekeeping frames, their "lineage" and "costs" of connectivity; for example:

- Name

- Current parent's name

- How many hops they are from the root node ("hop cost")

- "Toll cost" of using this propagator node (i.e., its availability)

  - Based on current processing power usage at propagator node

  - Based on number of active chirp end devices and propagator node descendants

  - Overall link quality (speed, reliability, etc.) of the path back to the root propagator node

Name-parentname-hoplevel-tollcost thus defines a broadcast beacon. Propagator node names are not globally unique; they are simply unique within a lineage subtree. Hence propagator node names, all the way up to the root, may be duplicated as long as the lineage path remains unique. Thus, two sibling propagator nodes may not share the same name, so a new propagator node with the same name as a current child propagator node will not be permitted to join that subtree.

The decision to join is then simplified to whether a prospective parent toll-cost/hop-cost ratio meets desired characteristics of current chirp packets that the prospective child propagator node would be transporting. The prospective incoming propagator node does not actually know what that data profile would be; it has not yet joined the network.

But it does potentially have access to chirp devices in its vicinity and can perform a rudimentary profile analysis, with the presumption that this is a representative sample set. Based on the profiling, if more latency is acceptable to the category of end device connected to the propagator node, a higher hop cost would be acceptable. Otherwise, a switch to a propagator node closer to the root, but at a higher toll cost, will be initiated. This is roughly an approximation of actual link quality when connected and having actual chirp devices connected to it.

It is tempting to suggest that the propagator node make a hasty connection and perhaps later, switch parents, but this is costly. Propagator nodes might then switch parents constantly, causing local oscillations (switching back and forth between subtrees), which eventually percolate to the top and decrease overall network efficiency substantially.

"Mother" propagator nodes (those with siblings) can therefore not "abandon the nest" while descendants are switching around; it would simply feed the chaos. Hence decay functions are built into the hierarchical control system that manages the network tree topology. Permission to switch parents travels at least as far up as the parent of both subtrees because both are being affected by the switch. If the child propagator nodes of those parents have settled down from a previous switch, permission is granted.

Scanning and Switching

In order to discover candidate parents, each relay propagator node must scan its environment periodically, preferably a broad scan covering multiple frequency and protocol "channels" available to the transceivers (again channels may be any type of wired or wireless link). If the propagator node has an additional dedicated scanning radio, its normal function of transporting chirps is not interrupted. Otherwise, the propagator node must request a scan "lunch break" from its parent to use its radios to scan on frequencies other than the one it is using for connection to the parent. At that point, it will need to tell its incoming link from its parent to "hold all messages." During that period, the end device clients are effectively temporarily disconnected, as shown in Figure 6-6.

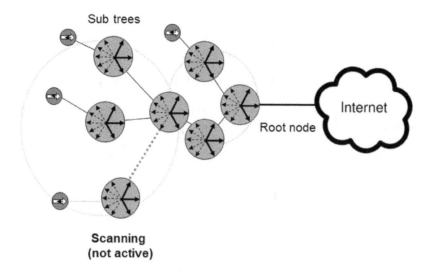

Figure 6-6. *Because each individual propagator node is responsible for finding its own best link to the IP connections, each must occasionally cease transmitting and receiving with its current "parent" to scan for alternative connections that might be of higher quality (higher speed, lower hop count, etc.). During these scanning periods, linked propagator nodes are instructed to hold traffic temporarily for the scanning node*

A parent propagator node would have multiple scan requests, which would be permitted in some weighted, round-robin manner, favoring child propagator nodes with more clients, for example. Using such a round-robin scheme, each sibling propagator node of a single parent would be granted a timed lunch break, so that no two siblings scan at the same time, thereby missing each other. The siblings may know of each other, but without mutual probe requests, they have little knowledge of the signal strength and tested link quality. Further, because the current "mother" parent's siblings (e.g., aunts) are also potential parent candidates, none of them may be in scan mode, either. Hence the scan request is being permitted by a parent's parent or grandmother. By the same token, the decision to allow a propagator node to switch is therefore also addressed by at least a grandparent to the requester propagator node.

In general, changes within a subtree (child moving from mother to aunt) will not affect the grandparent aggregated upstream throughput because both the aunt and mother are its children. So if the shift request is within the parent's siblings, the perturbation is contained and temporal. In general, it is at least grandmothers of the intended parent candidate who provide the final permissions.

For network topologies with less than a small number of hops, it is more efficient to let the root propagator node address both switch and scan requests. The root propagator node will generally have more processors and memory because it also handles the chirp-to-IP interface. As one of many "hubs" for the chirp data streams, it is also the logical place for publishing agents to reside (and perhaps collocated integrator functions).

Some of those publishing agents may want to have a say in the changes in network topology, so publishing agents may be part of the control plane managing the physical network. Because the physical network and logical network map to each other, the only option is to change the network topology by moving propagator node connections around, based on the global (root level) toll cost/hop cost criteria. The network topology is thus managed to be in dynamic alignment with end device traffic and subscriber demand.

As with "workers" in insect colonies, the primary function of every propagator node, all the way from the edges of the network to the root propagator node, is identical. Each wants to improve its lot, but with a view to long–term network stability. This is akin to ant or bee colonies, in which the common good affects all positively. Thus a propagator node may be directed by the root propagator node to switch parents because it would streamline the small data publishing flows. Or nodes may be directed to disassociate a chirping end device and have another sibling (aunt) adopt the orphan. So each of the sibling propagator nodes may, over time, become specialist hubs for end device category clusters and the social network coalesces towards more efficient routing. This is akin to trees changing their growth to adapt to changes in sun and shade. Adaptive network trees, like natural trees, are driven by the common good of the entire tree, including all constituents, down to the chirp end devices at the edges.

Specialized and Basic Routing

Although in many cases links between propagator nodes will be IP-based, the extensible chirp protocol may also be used between propagator nodes to provide information at various levels of granularity. Within the propagator node community there may be specialist propagator nodes that will connect only to other specialist relay propagator nodes. They may limit their relay efforts to specific chirp categories or classes of end devices, thereby forming a private and exclusive logical chirp network. These specialists may use other non-specialist propagator nodes to provide the transport and routing between other specialist propagator nodes, but in effect the meaning of the data being routed is accessible only intraspecialist.

In order to support routing requests from the wider community, all propagator nodes collaborate when possible in service to the larger network. Thus basic routing is part of a common protocol and language; extensions are specialist/publishing agent-based.

The basic routing is similar to Layer 2 wired Ethernet switch stacks and their wireless mesh node equivalents (see Figure 6-7). In both cases, the tree topology ensures scalable O(n) routing overhead. In each case, there is only one uplink. The "flatness" of Layer 2-based ("switched") networks eliminates the need for additional processing and protocols required of routed networks, such as the router-based global Internet.

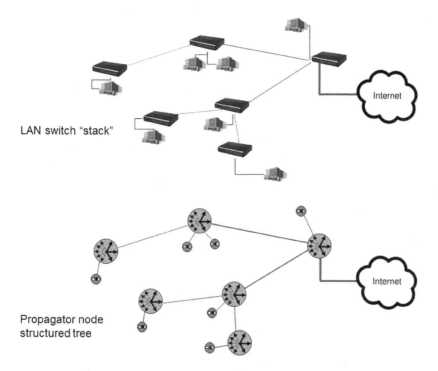

LAN switch "stack"

**Propagator node
structured tree**

Figure 6-7. In order to obtain reasonable routing efficiency without traditional routing overhead, the propagator node mesh is a flat structured tree, much like a "stack" of Ethernet local area network (LAN) switches. But unlike the LAN switch stack, distributed intelligence in each propagator node manages uplinks and downlinks to avoid loops while also maintaining alternative paths to allow for rerouting around failures

Housekeeping Frames for Network Intelligence

As noted earlier, the very basic "housekeeping" information that relay propagator nodes may transmit must minimally include the hop cost, toll cost, and parent name. The parent name is needed so that a prospective child can talk directly to the parent. Recall that the grandparent manages scan and switch events, so it knows whether a better parent is available, but is out to lunch performing a scan. A propagator node might be left awaiting association permission from a prospective parent node's parent until a scan is over. This delay ensures that after connections are made, they do not have to switch to a better candidate that is discovered after some later scans. The grandparent is being proactive.

Thus, the very basic housekeeping frame from all propagator nodes must contain:

- My name
- My parent name
- My hop level (from the root node)
- My toll cost

Newly powered–up or unconnected "orphan" propagator nodes send and receive probe requests from multiple connected nodes in their vicinity during their scanning period after power up. From these, the "orphan" propagator node can surmise which candidates are siblings, based on their parent name. Should it join any sibling, it is assured of collaborative alternatives within the same subtree (the aunts). This engenders its "survival" in terms of redundant paths with minimal changes; the rest of the subtree back to the root propagator node would be unchanged for between-sibling switches. Routing updates are needed only at the last hop. In contrast, switching between entire subtrees is more onerous, especially if that subtree's siblings are not available as backups. Survival favors joining subtrees with multiple accessible sibling mother/aunts.

Latency and Throughput Tradeoffs

Exchange of housekeeping frames enabled orphans to discover the presence of potential parents. Potential parents' relative proximity is measured during probe requests to determine effective link quality, which is included with topology analysis in the selection process. The total available throughput in a string-of-pearls link is simply that of the weakest link–the link with the worst "performance".

Candidate parents may thus receive pings to test aggregate link quality all the way up to the root propagator node. In general, each propagator node has an inherent predilection to choose the best "lineage" to connect with. But there are tradeoffs. Ideally, all things being equal, propagator nodes would want to connect as close to root propagator nodes as possible because Internet of Things traffic is largely upstream. However, the link quality of a direct wireless connection to a lower-hop-count but physically more-distant propagator node may be much worse than routing through more intermediary propagator nodes.

In the previous examples, overall back haul throughput from all upstream traffic to the root degrades as the tree topology is modified by toll-cost and hop-cost ratios favoring low hop cost (as shown on the right of Figure 6-8). But when the toll cost of lower-speed links is considered, the topology at left in Figure 6-8 is actually more efficient overall.

High speed links in blue, lower-speed links in red

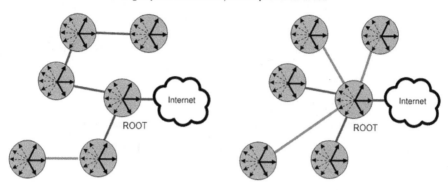

Higher hop cost, but better performance   Lower hop cost, but poorer performance
                                                 through lower-speed links

Figure 6-8. *Although lower hop cost (fewer node-to-node links) is a first-order approximation of best overall performance (on the right), sometimes lower speed link paths (due to distance, perhaps) make a higher-hop-count topology more efficient (on the left)*

In addition to overall link quality ascertained through pings, the availability of the candidate parent to service additional requests drives the final decision. Great overall backhaul throughput is academic if the node is already saturated, based on its limited processing power. Toll cost provides information to the nodes regarding levels of availability. Higher-toll-cost propagator nodes are being selective, mindful of their own limitations and therefore protecting their existing clients from being crowded out. Thus allegiances are formed, wherein propagator nodes develop preferences to belong to particular subtrees that demonstrate healthy characteristics (e.g., multiple sibling accessibility, etc.)

Routing Table Updates

Having joined the network, propagator nodes must now begin relaying chirp broadcasts in their vicinity. Propagator nodes would typically have one uplink to maintain the tree structure, although multiple uplinks servicing disparate trees (to avoid cycles) are also permitted. Multiple downlinks can service both chirp and IP traffic on both the same and distinct wireless interfaces. The uplinks could be either chirp- or IP-based (e.g., Wi-Fi or Ethernet).

For each disparate uplink, routing tables are maintained that provide Layer 2 switching network functionality. Packets are moved either up the tree or down the tree via the immediate children, along the tree branches. The decision is based on a condensed routing table, updated by each propagator node, based on a full housekeeping frame sent periodically and circulated within the relevant subtree.

Each housekeeping frame is tagged with a counter number. Because housekeeping frames will travel multiple paths in broadcasts, propagator nodes ensure that the same counter number is not rebroadcast. Further, each propagator node (and its publishing agent, if so equipped) may decide how far up or down the tree to provide the broadcast. For example, a parent switch to sibling aunt requires no further broadcasts than the last hop routing table.

Eventually, each propagator node is aware of the following:

- Its own immediate children

- In the case of relay propagator nodes, their children, and so on

- Adjacent propagator nodes that may serve as alternate parents

- Its current overall current link quality and throughput

- Through scanning, the overall link quality of alternate parents

Over time, the cost of switching back and forth is reduced by developing more data on the current parent and on its alternatives. This information leads to stable networks at the local levels.

The routing table is available to all members of the current subtree to (at least) the level of a grandparent. Each propagator node is aware of is entire subtree of descendants below it, at least two hops down. After that, the knowledge is somewhat irrelevant because its grandchildren, on having the packets delivered to them, will know how to relay them further. All the grandparent needs to know is *roughly* where the chirp parent propagator node resides—the portion of its descendant subtree (a general direction of routing suffices). If chirp devices move around, one or two packets intended for them will be lost (recall that there is no retry or retransmission in chirps). For each chirp descendant under its care, propagator nodes need to be aware only of the following:

- The chirp device descendant's immediate parent propagator node

- The location of that parent propagator node within its subtree (e.g., lineage)

- That the lineage path from the root propagator node to chirp device exists

Some chirps will be picked up by multiple propagator nodes, and each will rebroadcast the packets in the directions specified by the arrow of transmission. However, in each case it will tag the packet with the chirp device's immediate propagator node, which is the last part of a lineage tree. Multiple chirp packets will thus travel separately upstream through different relay paths, from multiple propagator nodes that pick up the chirps in their vicinity. Multiple lineage paths are available.

Multiple paths are useful when redundancy is desirable. Such is *not the case* with chirp sensor data (given the relative unimportance of any single chirp), so pruning of multiple paths is performed at the grandparent level. Chirp packets are relayed through one node only, typically the node closest to it and therefore the best link quality. Others, also picking up the chirps directly from the devices, are directed to ignore those chirps. The chirp device is now assigned a unique lineage or relay path back to the root. Thus, even in the case of unidirectional chirp streams, an association is made to prune redundant traffic.

The Power of Local Agents and Integrator Functions

When local publishing agents are added to propagator nodes, a tree-based, scalable, hierarchy-driven control system emerges. Filters are applied to progressively reduce redundant data upstream and to define preferred routes or destinations. Here is the beginning of small data flows, as chirp data being sent upstream continues to be more refined as it passes through multiple rule–based logical sieves.

As streams of chirps travel upstream toward the IP root in this model of the Internet of Things, agents within propagator nodes at strategic (often branching) locations along the route may perform local pruning, aggregation, and exception handling, thereby reducing the traffic and improving load performance. Because multiple agents can be operating on the same data, some form of collaborative scheduling and sharing of timing requirements is needed.

Task Scheduling within the Internet of Things

In the emerging Internet of Things' three-tiered architecture, propagator nodes manage the flow of aggregated and pruned data between end devices and integrator functions. When these propagator nodes incorporate a publishing agent (and the requisite IP interface), they may have access to two vital pieces of information supplied by integrator functions that are the receivers in the publish/subscribe framework. This information includes the following:

- **For routing:** The location of the integrator function that is in search of data characterized by its specific category or originating location (the publish/subscribe "neighborhood" described in Chapter 5)

- **For scheduling priority:** Timing requirements for delivery of the data (outdated data may have no value and need not be propagated through the network), along with estimates of time required for data to reach integrator functions

Communication between integrator functions and publishing agents takes place over the IP interface using standard Representational State Transfer (RESTful) or Simple Object Access Protocol (SOAP) protocols.

Through their exchange of housekeeping frames and observed traffic routing delays, propagator nodes are aware of how much time is taken moving packets across their managed chirp network, across the chirp-to-IP bridge. On the chirp side, latency is more deterministic: a simple count of the number of hops to the root node defines, in large part, the delay. On the IP side, things are more complex because the IP highway is being shared by other devices from other communities.

Propagator nodes are, however, in periodic communication with destination IP addresses. Simple ACK protocols within the RESTful API can provide current or predicted estimates of IP traffic. Working backward, propagator nodes back-calculate when chirp bus loads should leave. This feeds the collaborative scheduling and stack management routines. The scheduler may also drive aggregation (bulking) to ensure an equitable compromise between bus size, its frequency, and the IP cost at different times.

Smaller bus loads will leave more frequently for passengers in a rush; others will be compensated by a lower bus price for travelling on larger but less frequent departures. Some buses may arrive earlier, others later, but the schedule stacking is usually managed proactively. Supply and demand of the chirp packets and their arrival is driven by dynamic subscriber demands. This is a dynamic form of prioritizing, based on chirp useful life and subscriber demand information generated by the integrator function(s).

Higher-level Interchange

Similar standard IP-based protocols are used between integrator functions and filter gateways, as well as to create relationships among two or more integrator functions as neighborhoods and affinities are created, modified, and abandoned over time based on known and discovered data sources.

As noted in Chapter 5, integrator functions may be collocated with propagator nodes in some applications. These distributed integrator functions may be relatively simple, but their strength lies in numbers and their ability to support multiple interpretations of the same data. Distributed integrator functions in this scenario initiate corresponding actions with significantly lower latency than if everything were sent round-trip to distant integrator functions. There are situations in which chirp data needs must propagate all the way up, but like the Mars Rover, when latency matters, some level of local autonomy is essential to the survival of a network burdened at the edges.

THE POWER OF PUBLISHING AGENTS

An example illustrates the savings in IP traffic and improvement in responsiveness for a 100-sensor network. Consider, for simplicity, a ten-node string of pearls chain, with each relay propagator node supporting ten sensors, all the way back up to the root. For example, these sensors could be part of an underground coal mining tunnel, with propagator nodes forming the lifeline for both IP and chirp traffic.

Simple rule-based logic in distributed integrator functions watches the methane gas occurrence across the tunnel. The development of methane in one region could also affect adjacent regions, so a blob of methane gas publishers may appear abruptly and unexpectedly.

Sending such "exception handling" upstream to big data servers is clearly valuable. It is questionable whether routine and acceptable readings would be transmitted. But without some local handling, there may be no way of defining an exception, without a base line of routine readings. Hence publishing agents may also maintain some short history.

In lower-end and consumer versions of propagator nodes, there would be limited agents available—most data may be pushed upstream to parent propagator nodes and on to separate integrator functions. But multihop paths and their associated latency may be unacceptable for some mission-critical enterprise applications. In a previous era, Programmable Logic Controllers (PLCs) wired to sensors and actuators on the factory floor, managed the deluge of real-time, latency-sensitive machine-to-machine traffic, escalating only that which fell out of their rule-based relay ladder logic diagrams used by PLCs. Today, that same approach can be applied to rule-based agents residing on propagator nodes, close to the sensor/actuators. This reduces latency for enterprise class machine-to-machine communications.

Managing Multiple Isochronous Relationships

As introduced in Chapter 5, regardless of whether device communication is IP- or chirp-based, independent control loops (with publishing agents as intermediaries acting as the translation mechanisms between the upper and lower control loops) are inherently more efficient than round-tripping. Some devices, such as smartphones, are inherently chirp-capable (e.g., IR and Wi-Fi) and can participate in both control loops, acting like a bridge between the two banks of the river, each with its own control loops.

Beyond round-trip latency considerations, there is a more fundamental reason for this tiered control and communications model. The language and vocabulary of end devices is fundamentally divergent from that at the big data server level. Sensors publish their limited view of the world, whereas big data provides insights into a more comprehensive world view, incorporating multiple sensor streams, past history, future trends, and so on. Because function dictates language and vocabulary, some form of translation is required—one cannot expect purpose-built machinery to communicate directly without translation.

In the contemporary IP-based thin-client model, any translation of data to a format palatable to big data consumers must take place *before* sensor data enters the IP network. Needless to say, that puts the onus on the end devices and their machine-to-machine communication protocols to be intelligible. What was a terse, purpose-built dialect now has to be interpreted in a device-abstracted language. Agents and their location within the local control loop reduce this burden, as shown in Figure 6-2.

An Organic Solution for the IoT

One cannot always know, *a priori*, the type of categories of interest for specific integrator functions, any more than winds can always provide focused beams of pollen to their awaiting subscribers. Some discovery is needed, though; at the very least, notification from "mother" propagator nodes that a new category of sensor chirps has become active in a geo location under its care (e.g., a subtree of the network). Notification summaries of sensor activity would therefore be periodically provided. Interested integrator function subscribers can then direct their publishing agents within propagator nodes (if available) to provide the level of granularity/aggregation/pruning/exception handling needed to optimize data gathering.

Over time, an agent-based, machine-to-machine social network emerges, tapping into the full richness of data offered by the Internet of Things.

CHAPTER 7

■ ■ ■

Examples and Applications

Lots of information about Internet of Things applications has been published to date, but virtually all these examples assume a continuation of *current* networking architecture models. Specifically, IPv6 extended to the very edge of the network, with end devices powerful enough (in terms of processor, memory, etc.) to run an IP protocol stack. But as has been described in preceding chapters, this architecture is unsuitable for the "next wave" of IoT end devices to be brought onto the network. They will simply be too cheap, too numerous, too hard to manage, and too varied to support the traditional networking model.

Another incorrect assumption made about the future of the Internet of Things is that the *data* models will remain much the same as today: well-defined, one-to-one relationships between IP–equipped end devices and big data servers at the core of a network accessed over the "cloud." But this traditional approach cannot *fully exploit* the potential richness and power of the IoT for a number of reasons:

- Data handling and storage at the big data servers

- Impracticalities of end-to-end control loops

- Inability to exploit a publish/subscribe world made up of neighborhoods and affinities of end devices

This chapter will first explore the impact each of these issues has on potential new IoT applications and then provide specific examples of new potential IoT applications.

Controlling the Cacophony

Machine-to-machine data interchanges are currently tedious: all raw, device-specific data must first be sanitized and then formatted to conform to big data representation schemes based on application programming interfaces (APIs) such as Representational State Transfer (REST) or Simple Object Access Protocol (SOAP). Next, the IP-stack-based transceivers on current end devices must send the data without collision with other IP device traffic, often using Carrier Sense Multiple Access with Collision Avoidance/ Detection (CSMA/CA or CSMA/CD). This is a lot of work for a simple temperature sensor, with its restricted and terse purpose-built vocabulary.

The users of big data are interested in an integration of small data: the device-abstracted, protocol-abstracted information streams. The onus of converting sensor raw data to big, data-friendly "small" data cannot be easily delegated to every end device as has been imagined to date for the Internet of Things. Managing diverse device driver interfaces and their specific interfaces and protocols rapidly spins out of control at the scope of the emerging IoT.

As the number of edge devices proliferates, the network effects of the traffic generated by billions of publishers and subscribers overwhelms the processor and memory processor enhancements enabled by Moore's Law (which is linear), as shown in Figure 7-1. Recall that machine-to-machine communities and their interactions are more akin to social networks; in other words, they are Metcalfe's Law or $O(n^2)$ (Order-*n*-Squared)-based. The data processing, storage, and networking requirements for cloud-based IoT analysis and control services will not be able to keep up with the deluge of small data emanating from the edges of the network. (They can barely keep pace, even in today's simplified and managed end-to-end thin-client IP applications.)

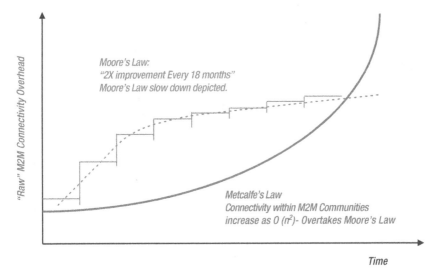

Figure 7-1. *Much of the current thinking on the Internet of Things assumes that constant hardware improvements (due to Moore's Law) will allow traditional networking schemes to be extended to the IoT. But in fact, the machine social network will grow much faster (Metcalfe's Law) and will require a more specialized architecture*

This will be true either for chirp-based networks or legacy IP end devices; the amounts of data are simply too great. For this reason, the emerging IoT architecture removes the overhead of the task of aggregating and transporting data from *both* the end devices *and* the big data servers. It instead segregates it within propagator nodes that can be deployed near the edges of the network (refer to Chapter 4).

Intelligence Near the Edge

The emerging Internet of Things architecture also provides for migration of intelligence toward the edge of the network in the form of publishing agents within the propagator nodes and/or distributed integrator functions. Through these capabilities, IoT applications may rely on these distributed intelligences to manage the conversion of chirp data streams to and from end devices such as sensors and actuators to small data flows that are more easily consumed by the big data integrator functions. This process will enable the rapid proliferation of a dizzying variety of applications using very simple, low-cost, or intermittently available end devices that are simply not possible with traditional IP networking schemes.

Incorporating Legacy Devices

An added benefit of this architecture is that applications requiring more-sophisticated end devices that *do* justify the cost and complexity of IP on board (video surveillance, for example) may also use the same architecture, easing the load on big data servers and making possible the extended publish/subscribe network of neighborhoods and affinities (see the following sidebar). The core objective is to encourage and manage a more equitable *division* of labor, one that only improves with time, as devices at the edge are permitted to be simpler in function. Simpler devices will rapidly proliferate at the edge once a supporting network infrastructure is in place that can both manage chirp streams on behalf of the end devices *and* create small data flows suitable for the benefit of big data integrator functions. See the following "Nailing a License Plate to a Stump" sidebar.

NAILING A LICENSE PLATE TO A STUMP

Many of today's Internet of Things commentators have hailed the address expansion incorporated within IPv6 as the solution for the IoT. And it is certainly mathematically true that IPv6 creates more than 340 undecillion (more than 3.4×10^{38}) potential addresses, which some have said is enough to assign one to every atom on the surface of the earth. (For logistical reasons, the practical limit is likely much less.) But compared with the roughly 4 billion unique addresses possible with IPv4, that is indeed a substantial improvement and certainly sufficient to address every potential end device in any conceivable Internet of Things.

But this analysis confuses addresses with functionality. It would certainly be possible to nail an automobile license plate to a tree stump (see Figure 7-2), which would make the stump uniquely identifiable and thus potentially addressable. But it does not magically enable the stump to drive away on the highway like a car. It is obviously missing the horsepower (a motor), means of transportation (wheels), and intelligence (a driver) to make any usefulness on the highway impossible.

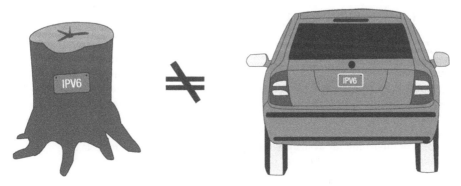

Figure 7-2. *Addressing is not performance*

In the same way, the capability to address an end device sensor or actuator is only a small part of the issue in the IoT. Without burdening the end device with horsepower (memory and processor), means of transportation (IP stack), and intelligence (central management and oversight), its data cannot make it to the "information superhighway," either.

Thus, the IPv6 address space alone doesn't solve the essential application problem in the IoT: enabling the connection of billions of end devices that are too simple to support full networking. The new emerging architecture of the Internet of Things creates the simple chirp structure that allows for the development of applications without demanding untenable requirements at the end devices.

Staying in the Loop(s)

One of the key challenges of extending legacy IP architectures to the Internet of Things is the inherent constraint created by using a protocol originally developed for host-to-host communications (peer-to-peer, by definition) to the very different and inherently asymmetrical world of the IoT. One of the impacts of this legacy on IoT applications is the difficulty of managing control loops over long distances and via the nondeterministic global Internet. Unlike a host-to-host interaction, IoT end devices and actuators often have very little or no intelligence of their own, so the task of managing them would fall to integrator functions accessed via some sort of round–trip control loop over a long-distance link.

Round-trip control via IP and the global Internet is an impractical means of controlling simple end devices at the extreme edges of the Internet of Things, especially because some may be only intermittently connected. Instead, localized control through distributed intelligence in nearby propagator nodes allows autonomous or semiautonomous control via on-board integrator functions or publishing agents (see Figure 6-2).

Given the delay and jitter (variation in delay) inherent in the global Internet, the existing IP network is a cumbersome and ultimately impractical solution for control of myriad simple end devices, as shown previously. But (as described in Chapter 6) the emerging IoT allows the control loops to be *decoupled* and thus become *isochronous*. An efficient lower-level local control loop may be in place between the propagator node and end device, whereas occasional updates and exceptions are communicated upstream to subscribed integrator functions. In turn, "tuning" and configuration messages may occasionally be received from integrator functions for implementation at the local end device actuator.

Okay on their Own

This multilevel control will allow for IoT applications that may function substantially autonomously in real time most of the time, including for extended periods when out of communication with a distant integrator function. This option of a much more rapid response from a local publishing agent or integrator function is a key feature of the emerging Internet of Things for autonomous and semiautonomous (advise and consent) tasks.

This distribution of intelligence throughout the emerging IoT architecture bodes well for its future. More autonomy means less supervisory control and less drain on resources required for round-tripping. The predictive elements (integrator functions) become more seasoned at being proactive, and reactive elements give way to proactive behavior. The overall system evolves to be more predictive, lean, and agile.

All the World Is a Subscription

Another legacy limitation of the host-to-host nature of IPv6 is that connections are inherently point-to-point between known devices. (Routers are required to create and manage these relationships.) This creates isolated "silos" of data, in that there are separate sets of end devices deployed for different functions. So in contrast with the emerging IOT, they may not be able to contribute their information to an integrator function, even if the combination would provide much more powerful information.

As described in Chapter 5, the emerging Internet of Things architecture is not limited by the concept of preset device-to-device relationships. Instead, integrator functions will create information neighborhoods made up of a wide variety of small data flows forwarded by propagator functions from many chirp data streams. The lowly chirp-enabled sensor is now a participant of the connected world, without changing its fundamentally simple function of publishing a specific category of real-time, raw, simply formatted data.

Exploring Affinities

Many new classes of IoT applications will be possible, in which integrator functions seek out potentially useful information by examining affinities between many publishing sources (see Figure 7-3). An example of this is temperature, pressure, and vibration; or small data streams that seem to vary in relationship to one another, or in relationships to an Internet data source, such as weather reports. Again, this would be more difficult in the traditional IP point-to-point environment, in which different device types tend to be segregated from one another.

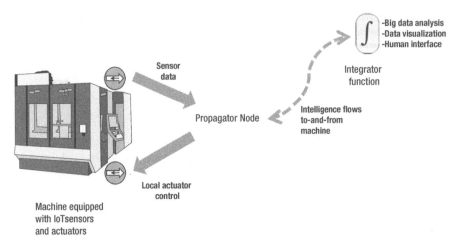

Figure 7-3. *Unlike traditional networks, many important and illuminating relationships may be unknown at the time of installation of an Internet of Things application. But over time, integrator functions may expand their "neighborhood" of information sources by exploring other data streams that share some affinities with the existing neighborhood of data sources. These new sources may be included for a time to "test" their usefulness, and may be later dropped or replaced and new sources explored*

In a world in which the data emanating from many IoT applications may be marked as public small data streams by their owners, the potential exists for incredible insights and efficiencies of scale as integrator functions build extensive subscriptions. The key aspect setting these applications apart from legacy Internet of Things applications built on traditional IPv6 networking is that the relationships between end devices and integrator functions may be unknown at the outset. Instead, they are built and refined over time by the integrator functions. A larger social network for data exchange emerges. The data streams will span the gamut: chirp sensory data, changing subscriber patterns, preferred data routing paths on specific days, and so on. End devices, propagator nodes, and the publishing agents within will "belong" to multiple "information social networks" informed by neighborhoods of subscribed data.

Social Machines

The information social networks will be free to grow to quite large sizes simply because machines are not constrained by Dunbar's Number (which theoretically limits the maximum interactions that humans can actively support to fewer than 200). Freed from legacy-style, predefined peer-to-peer interactions with thousands (or millions) of end devices by the distribution of networking intelligence and decoupling of control loops, integrator functions will be able to digest unprecedented amounts of distilled and directed data (see Figure 7-4).

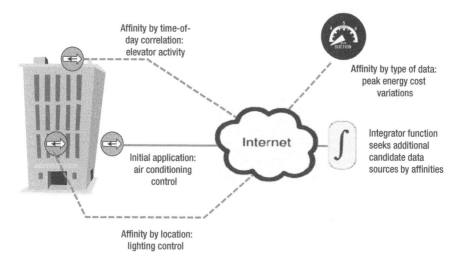

Propagator node network not shown for clarity

Figure 7-4. *Distributed networking capabilities in an ever-expanding mesh of propagator nodes will provide more and more refinement in pruning and tuning of chirp data streams to create more efficient small data flows. This growing efficiency will allow integrator functions to analyze more end points with less processing of individual data packets. The IoT will become more useful as the architecture expands*

From the machine-to-machine IoT perspective, intelligence is inferences drawn over time from multiple and diverse data sources. The proliferation over time of more and varied chirp–enabled end devices and propagator nodes will continue to expand the available universe of potentially interesting data streams. As more propagator nodes are added with the growth of the Internet of Things, the overall application data exchange flow rates will continue to improve linearly through the proactive use of pruning/ aggregation/exception handling, as shown previously. But the Metcalfe's Law network effect of the *information* will be growing even more rapidly in an $O(n^2)$ relationship.

Agriculture

Managing an agricultural enterprise is a difficult, multivariate endeavor; many man-made and natural factors are in play. In Figure 7-5, a lower–level local control loop applied by a distributed integrator function autonomously "manages" the actuators controlling the irrigation system valves (when they turn on or off, based on local moisture level sensors). This isochronous loop monitors and controls the amount of water applied locally within specific zones, avoiding over- or under-watering. But there is no need for round-trip control by a distant higher-level integrator function or for burdening a distant integrator function with a continuous stream of data from local moisture sensors.

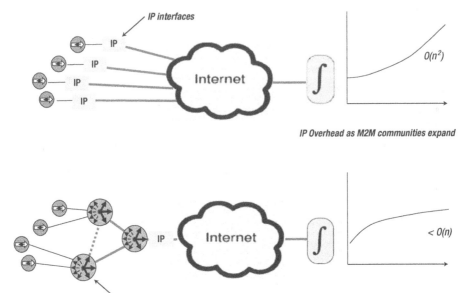

Figure 7-5. *A wide variety of sensors and other data sources combine to optimize yields and profitability from a farm field. Although lower-level control loops might monitor and manage irrigation through distributed integrator functions, additional integrator functions deployed at a "higher" level may take a wider variety of information into their analysis*

In the less-than-perfect world, however, patterns of water *absorption* by the crops are not easily discernible by these lower-level control loops. An airborne drone equipped with appropriate sensors (such as infrared) may be deployed to scan the corn field and collect a more global view of the terrain and where more water may be needed. The drone provides this information through its wireless interfaces to a smartphone or other general-purpose processor running an integrator function operating at a "higher" level than the moisture-sensor-irrigation-valve control loop. The integrator function correlates this to the current sprinkler map and fine-tunes it to ensure more even water distribution. Farmers may also be provided with suggestions regarding changing the terrain to provide slopes for more efficient irrigation. A few weeks later, the drone conducts another survey. Over time, the lower control loop, in conjunction with the upper control loop, generates a more comprehensive view of its region of interest.

The cost of one sophisticated but "remote" sensor (the drone) may be lower than implanting multiple simpler moisture sensors. The control loop is still being closed, and the drone and sensor ensemble is more modular, reusable, and upgradeable. Economies of scale kick in. The drone may be used by a farming community, a shared resource. If the control loop is being monitored weekly, the same drone can be used to close multiple control loops in adjoining farms. A swarm of such drones can be used to cover large areas in a low-cost, scalable manner.

The integrator functions may also discover and subscribe to a variety of other data streams and sources to create a richer combination of information. Weather forecasts, spot produce prices, the current cost of transportation, the availability and cost of contract field workers, and many other factors may be taken into account. Some of these other data streams will not be generated through the farmers' own efforts, but made available by others with public markers on the data streams. Trend analysis of these factors over time may point to the ideal moment to harvest the crop for maximum profits. The community of farmers, through shared resources and the integration of many data sources (some unforeseen at the time the application was first deployed), can compete more effectively with those in other regions.

SHOW ME YOUR DATA; I'LL SHOW YOU MINE

The previous farming example suggests that the group shares information of similar type for a similar goal: all are farmers in a specific area. But because the emerging Internet of Things architecture is fundamentally based on a publish/subscribe model, the creators and consumers of data streams may not be always have as much (or anything) in common. For example, a restaurant owner might want to know about foot traffic in a nearby shopping mall in order to target ads for video kiosks or instant coupons on social media. A trucking company might want to know about unusual traffic patterns created by an accident and detected by in-pavement or video-intersection sensors in order to reroute their fleet.

These and many more as-yet-unimagined opportunities may exist for sharing of data streams that are already being created. A nonmonetary "exchange" market place might emerge—or even one based on market pricing or auction models. Because the chirp protocol is category-based and publish-friendly, chirp streams and small data flows from nonaligned organizations can be acted upon. A key enabler of these potential exchanges is that the entire IoT architecture is oriented toward a publish/subscribe model rather than defined peer-to-peer relationships, even at the lowest levels. The chirps from the simplest sensor can be shared with an unlimited number of integrator functions without any change or reconfiguration required.

Home Health Care

The agricultural example described cooperative use of a population of Internet of Things sensors and actuators by defining information neighborhoods of related elements and seeking out affinities of potentially related and pertinent information. But other IoT applications will be more restrictive in their deployment and operation. The need for secure, private, and purpose-built communications will proliferate within local machine-to-machine communities.

In Figure 7-6, a small private IoT community of "vital signs" sensors feeds into a local integrator function for analysis and pattern matching near the network edge (the patient). Proactive monitoring and management of medication dosage and/or additional home care is also logically delegated to a private patient's home via additional sensors or inputs from a caregiver's smartphone.

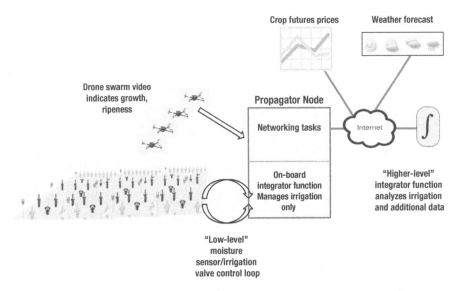

Figure 7-6. *A home heath IoT application might use a variety of sensors and other inputs, including wearables and ingestibles, to create a complete picture of a convalescing patient's condition. Local alarms may be triggered for particular threshold readings or combinations of conditions and events. Periodic regular reports and occasional exceptions may be forwarded to off-site medical personnel for emergent response or long-term analysis*

Because individual sensors need not be burdened with the processor, power, and memory overhead required to support IPv6, they might be smaller, lighter, cheaper, and less invasive, which could include wearable and ingestible form factors. With the local analysis enabled by the emerging Internet of Things architecture, readings from many sensors may be considered together, along with variables such as room temperature and time of day, allowing a more-sophisticated combined analysis rather than simply alarming on one boundary condition.

This private information neighborhood becomes adaptive and self-learning to provide the first-tier reporting and response initiation autonomously. If the patient's heart rate or breathing becomes erratic, the patient and caregiver will know immediately based on alarms and other feedback devices triggered by the local integrator function. Notice of the exception condition would also be transmitted to distant medical personnel, who are made aware of it immediately. The stimulus-response is more proactive, potentially averting or reducing the severity of an event. Round-trip communication to a distant integrator function is now restricted to escalated issues only.

Safe and Efficient Process Control

Natural resource– and commodities-processing enterprises such as oil refineries present a demanding "analog" application. Maintaining liquid flow rates, temperatures, and pressures may be critical to ensuring higher yields of end products. Keeping values within tolerances may help avoid leaks and spills, mitigating environmental impacts, and government fines; not to mention worker and public safety. Environmental monitoring sensors (air, water, vibration, etc.) can also help keep the plant operating within required specifications.

In these types of applications, the more data that can be gathered at more points, along with autonomous or semiautonomous feedback loops allowing for control of actuators such as valves and vents, the better. Chirp-based sensors can be smaller, cheaper, more rugged, and demand less power than traditional IP-based devices, allowing them to be deployed in greater numbers and with less management and technical support. Redundancy through sheer number of sensors is a corollary benefit.

As with other applications, lower-level control loops might allow near-instantaneous response to local factors, such as actuating a valve to reduce the flow of ingredients to moderate a chemical reaction that is exceeding norms, with only exceptions sent "up the line" for additional monitoring and analysis. This would be much more efficient than requiring a round–trip data exchange for small adjustments.

A "carpet" of moisture sensors below key pipes and junctions might detect leaks at their earliest stages, long before they would be otherwise noticed. Footfall, wireless, or infrared sensors might help track personnel to ensure safe practices and operations, as well as to allow rapid response and rescue in case of an emergency.

Another advantage of deploying a wide variety of sensors in large numbers is the capability to analyze data flows from many devices. A neighborhood of interest might include liquid detectors, temperature monitors, and vibration sensors. Combinations of changing readings might pinpoint a future maintenance problem such as a worn bearing that is leaking slightly, a bit hotter than normal, and creating a small vibration in the equipment. Recognizing this state earlier allows work to be scheduled without excessive downtime, even when no individual sensor type showed out-of-tolerance readings on its own.

Better Perimeter Security and Surveillance

Facilities are only as secure as their most vulnerable access point. One way to increase security is again to increase the number of points being monitored. A field of footfall sensor "motes" is impractical if each must be burdened with the overhead of a full IP networking stack. It would be impractical to wire them all, and a combination of solar and battery power might be enough to drive simple chirp logic (see Figure 7-7).

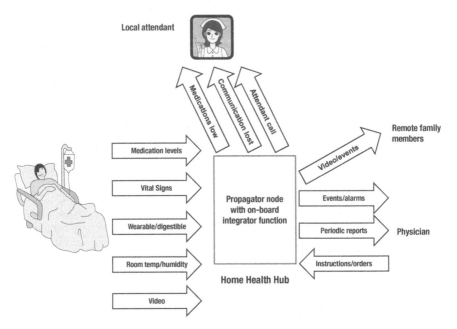

Figure 7-7. *In the emerging IoT architecture, networking demands on end device sensors are minimal, enabling many more of them (both in type and sheer number) to be "seeded" into the environment to improve installation security*

As "swarming" algorithms become more sophisticated, very simple airborne or ground drones might help patrol vulnerable areas of the perimeter. Autonomous local coordination of drone travel (along specific routes, in response to detected potential breaches, etc.) could be combined with the propagation of alert and alarm messages as dictated by the situation.

Similarly, video camera "swarms," operating in coordinated manner, could track/ follow persons of interest as necessary. A camera swarm might collectively focus its attention to look for particular patterns or people. The cameras may be stationary, but through handoffs to others in the shared network, they still effectively provide ubiquitous surveillance coverage. In places where cameras are not deployed, mobile units with cameras will provide the needed continuity. Video surveillance will operate seamlessly as mobile and stationary cameras are employed as members of a collective intelligence community.

As discussed in Chapter 5, because integrator functions are IP-based, they may incorporate native IP data streams from more sophisticated cameras and sensors, combining these with small data flows aggregated by propagator nodes from chirp device streams. A single point of analysis and control thus manages both legacy and emerging devices. They might include biohazard, radiation, and other threat sensors.

Faster Factory Floors

With the increasing automation of the factory floor, the autonomous or semiautonomous lower-level control and feedback loops made possible through distributed intelligence within the Internet of Things may allow for higher production and better use of human resources. If integrator functions can handle lower-level adjustments and controls of operating machinery, human eyes and minds may be freed for longer-term analysis and optimization, based on exception and historical data collected at a higher level.

Machine autodiagnosis, parts supplies and quality, temperature and emission sensing all can be combined with video analysis of production lines and conveyers to maximize efficiency. As with some other applications, a key benefit of the emerging Internet of Things is the potential small size and cost of chirp-based end devices, allowing for much broader usage.

For example, industrial robots in factory automation are increasingly equipped with force and vision sensing for adaptive motion control. They are capable of stopping upon encountering an obstacle without damaging themselves or the obstacle. Factory floor environments that once needed to be rigidly structured (to ensure that "dumb" robots operated safely) are now more flexible in their designs with sensor-guided control.

Mobile robots, as in Automatic Guided Vehicles (AGVs) previously were required to move on preset paths, following lines inlaid or painted on the floor. More AGVs now use location markers on passageways and real=time data from other AGVs to collaboratively determine collision-free trajectories in factories with no markings on the floor. Sensor-driven path planning in real time in untaught factory floor environments is now practical; it was unthinkable only a decade ago. As more IoT sensor end devices become part of smart buildings, the character of industrial robots will continue to become more adaptive to changes in the environment. This will significantly reduce the cost of preplanned factory automation infrastructure.

True Home Automation

A new class of home and enterprise Access Points (APs) will be developed with the appropriate end device chirp transceiver built in, as shown in Figure 7-8. These will support both legacy Wi-Fi (IP) and chirp communications, and will typically include an IoT propagator node and (often) a publishing agent or an integrator function. These ambidextrous devices will appear as two logically distinct devices, even if they are using the same transceivers (for example, 2.4GHz unlicensed band radios). Thus each of these chirp-aware APs in the house, part of a mesh network, can provide access to all publishers and subscribers within the home legacy and Internet of Things communities. Each node and its agents can be regulated by a supervisory control system, which can move agents, remove them, update them, and so on.

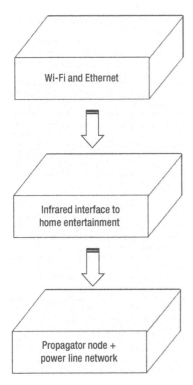

Figure 7-8. *In home and small office environments, attractive modular packaging will allow consumers to "build up" combinations of needed functions based on a "base" propagator node with IP functionality mated to additional transceivers to serve new and legacy devices. These "stacks" would often include a local integrator function serving as the home automation hub. This hub would be accessed wirelessly by an app on a smartphone, tablet, or PC*

In actual packaging, propagator nodes may be stackable, as shown previously, supporting multiple interfaces and their disparate tree-like networks (e.g., Wi-Fi and chirp infrared). Device-specific agents would reside on the propagator node networks, specific to one type of transceiver interface and sensor type. This would encompass a tight low-level interface with language and protocol *specific* to the device and its function. Thus a temperature sensor need "know" nothing more than how to transmit its temperature over an IR link. If no transmission is received, its agent "knows" that something is amiss, not the device. Further, to simplify matters, only the publishing agent needs to know how to parse and read meaning into the terse chirp stream, pruning, aggregating, and forwarding small data flows toward integrator functions as appropriate.

Local home automation monitoring and control will take the form of an on-board integrator function. This might be managed by a front panel or (more likely) a smartphone/tablet/PC app and would provide an extensible means of interacting with all the devices in the home, whether chirp-based or legacy IP. This could easily expand to include alarm and home entertainment functions. There will also exist "translator" modules to permit non-Wi-Fi/non-chirp devices (such as TV remotes) to be incorporated as data sources or control points (much as a universal TV remote today). One of these modules will likely be a replacement for the home AC main plug. A simple chirp-based interface could provide information about energy usage and allow remote power-on/power-off.

Legacy translators such as these will be important for many years until Internet of Things–enabled devices replace current technology. Given that the life of some large appliances is 15 years (as opposed to 2–3 years for electronic technology), transition technologies are needed (see Figure 7-9).

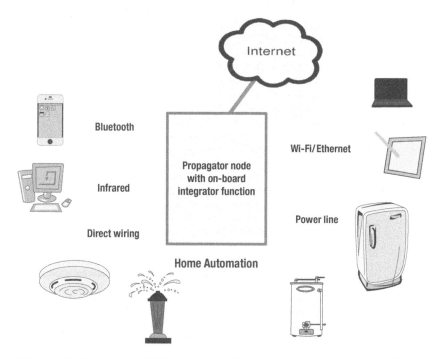

Figure 7-9. *The Internet of Things home hub brings together security, entertainment, activity monitoring, environmental comfort, energy usage and other interests within a single intelligent framework. Simple chirp protocols will suffice for the overwhelming majority of end devices in the home environment, but legacy IP and non-IP (e.g., TV remote) streams may also be supported*

This will bring about *true* home automation, with a variety of appliances, sensors, and other devices smoothly coordinated via a single point of intelligence, as discussed previously. The fabled Internet of Things toaster need not be burdened with a processor, memory, and an IP stack—a simple chirp interface will do. Physical interfaces may be varied, as noted in Chapter 2: Infrared, Bluetooth, Power Line, and other interfaces may all come together at the propagator node. Clusters of simple chirp devices, many not even yet imagined, will connect via these interfaces. Integrator functions will interpolate events and data, detecting movement in the house and adjusting heating and cooling zones, for example, or turning off lights in unused rooms.

IoT end devices will also be able to communicate tersely and cogently with external integrator functions, reaching these via the IP interface of the home propagator node and the home's high-speed broadband Internet link. For example, the trashcan might chirp its level of "fullness," which the home network relays to the garbage collection company. Trucks and arrival times are accurately scheduled.

In another example, kitchen appliances might transmit status to a contracted appliance maintenance-and-repair depot, which would in turn schedule a repair visit to cover multiple devices (as shown in Figure 7-10). A list of those repairs is made available to services in that locality, if permitted. The home user can also specify the schedules that suit her, as opposed to the other way around. The combined information is a "request for quote" sent to multiple repair service subscribers. One may be selected. The repairman's visit is scheduled/confirmed by the home user. Alternatively, she may choose to have the parts mailed to her and do it herself. Another set of electrical appliance retailers will present their bids.

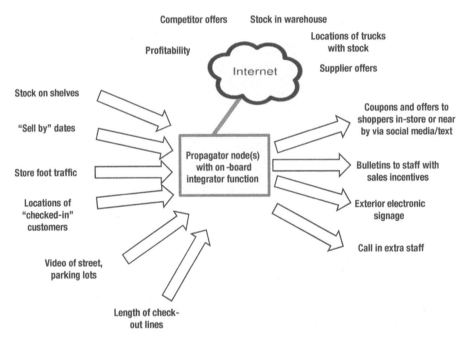

Figure 7-10. *Although many home automation IoT applications will be localized, the potential exists for end devices to update distant contracted organizations about their status and health. Maintenance reminders and service visits may be scheduled in response. Major appliance and equipment OEMs may offer these services to their own customers; others may offer a service supporting many different brands and types of equipment*

The IoT-enabled home may also coordinate with smart meters for gas and (especially) electric utilities to minimize usage during expensive time-of-day billing periods by throttling down or turning off some appliances and scheduling operations with an eye to maximum economies of cost and utility demand, as well as current and expected weather. Cooperative programs with utilities may offer additional price advantages if the utility is allowed to bias these decisions to match its generating capacities.

Wholesale and Retail: Beyond RFID

Dozens of Internet of Things applications have already been suggested and/or are being rolled-out now, both for online merchandisers and brick-and-mortar locations. To date, these applications have often been based on technologies such as Radio-Frequency Identification (RFID) along with IP-based readers and sensors. RFID chips are generally inert until powered-up by a nearby reader, so there may be many applications in which a simple chirp-based device will provide more functionality.

In the competitive world of retailing, well-stocked and properly "fronted" (products aligned to the shelf edge) displays are more enticing to shoppers. Low-cost, chirp-based sensors might be deployed along a shelf edge. Powered by overhead light, they might identify when product displays require attention. Or sensors in the floor or shoppers' carts might trigger coupon deals and other offerings based on location within the store.

Shoppers who have "checked-in" to a specific store on social media might welcome these offerings catered to their location and path through the store. As in an earlier example, foot or parking lot traffic might be used to gauge the type, number, and attractiveness of offers presented. After all, there's no need to offer major discounts at this moment if it is known that the parking lot is currently filling up. This is another area in which a variety of data streams, including factors such as current and expected weather, might be brought together by an integrator function for autonomous or semiautonomous action (see Figure 7-11).

Figure 7-11. *Combining data from many sources, a retailer might make available offers and coupons specifically related to stock on hand, store traffic, weather conditions, and many other factors*

In the back-end and wholesale environments, inexpensive and/or disposable (even biodegradable) shock and temperature sensors might monitor shipping conditions in transit and help track stock in the warehouse. Efficiently rotating stock based on first-in-first-out or expiration dates might be aided by more data from individual containers or cases. (And then there is the oft-told IoT tale of the refrigerator noticing that one is low on milk, seeing that one's location is near the store, and generating a text reminder to pick up a half-gallon on the way home.)

A Broader "Net" in Natural Sciences

As with the security examples noted previously, a larger number and great geographic spread of sensors is important for improving the usefulness of natural science observations. Strain and crack gauges spread over very large areas might allow better monitoring of geological conditions, perhaps leading to prediction capabilities for natural events such as earthquakes and volcanic eruptions. Detection of snow levels, CO_2 emissions (as from a wildfire), air and water pollution, and many other parameters may be much easier with cheaper, lighter, and more-easily-managed end devices. Small, cheap, solar-powered IoT chirp devices might allow scientists to cast broader nets for data than before.

Speaking of nets, wild and farmed animal populations (fish, cattle, birds, and so on) might also be monitored with implantable and/or digestible chirp devices. As with many other applications, the promiscuous forwarding built into the basic chirp architecture and the propagator node might allow recruitment of a very wide-ranging network of nonaligned propagator nodes as a "free" propagation medium for this data. This might allow a collection of data from far afield without the cost of building out a propagator node network specifically for one application. A sparse mesh network of "volunteer"

IP–capable propagator nodes (which are more power-hungry) will provide the networking path, but the underlying lower level of end devices will remain light and terse in their communication protocols.

Living Applications

Emerging IoT applications will be "alive" in the sense of being adaptive, self-healing, self-forming, and largely collaborative. The architectural foundations will together enable unprecedented innovation in the development and deployment of new applications in the Internet of Things:

- Minimal networking requirements for end devices

- Provision for local autonomy of action

- Distributed intelligence to offload both end devices and integrator functions

- A flexible publish/subscribe model creating neighborhoods of information

■ ■ ■

CHAPTER 8

Pathways to the Internet of Things

This book has described the details of an emerging new architecture for the Internet of Things. But new architectures rarely displace legacy systems unless there is an overarching benefit that drives their adoption. For the IoT, the major benefit can be expressed in the unique new relationships possible between the myriad end devices and the big data servers that analyze and control the data flowing to and from those end devices.

Data Drives a Change

Fundamentally, the coming billions of Internet of Things devices will simply generate *too much data* to be analyzed in traditional ways. Instead of the usual one-to-one predefined IP legacy topology, only a publish/subscribe model allows the big data servers to be selective and adaptive in the choice of data to operate upon, and is thus smarter over time.

Even more importantly, the big data analyzers will not even know what data streams would be useful *until they discover the data*. Information neighborhoods created through data stream affinities will present opportunities for selecting and combining small data flows from many different kinds of end devices, not all of which are even part of a specific application. This allows IoT applications to become smarter and smarter over time, as ever more end devices are installed (see Figure 7-4). Whatever initial purpose these end devices serve, they may also unexpectedly and unpredictably benefit other applications that discover their data outputs and find them useful (if the chirp streams are made public).

When initially installed, specific appliances, sensors, and actuators may serve a particular application. But over time, new end devices may be deployed by the same or other organizations. Data streams from these new devices may also be recognized by "affinities" of place, time, or correlation to be incorporated into the original application's information "neighborhood."

Classification is the Challenge, Chirp is the Answer

So if the only way that IoT can reach its potential is through (often) ad hoc publishing and subscription of data streams, what does that say about the data being sent and received by end devices? Simply put, that data must be *externally* classified so that future known and unknown subscribers can locate, identify, and act upon it. This is completely different from traditional IP networking, in which the external packet components are essentially generic, and thus any classification (moisture sensor versus streetlight versus toaster, and so on) must take place within the data payload itself. In essence, the packet structure of the chirps is *potential knowledge*; chirps are not merely the *containers* of information.

The self-describing classification inherent in the very structure of the chirp packet (refer to Chapter 6) is designed to make publish/subscribe relationships possible across applications, vendors, locations, and time. These self-describing classifications will identify characteristics that allow data subscribers to distinguish between all manner of sensors, actuators, and other devices. This is the prerequisite first step toward determining whether the data being generated by these devices is potentially useful and is necessary to make possible a publish/subscribe network with the eventual scope of the Internet of Things.

The power of self-classified data streams is the fundamental driver of a new emerging IoT architecture. (Even if IP capability in all devices were free, *and it's not*, there would remain a need for a set of commonly understood self-classifications carried within the IP packet payload to enable broad publish/subscribe utility, as shown in Figure 8-1. (See the following "Chirps in IP Packets? Why?" sidebar.) The steps of implementing the network architecture needed to create and transport these self-classified data streams are the subject of this chapter.

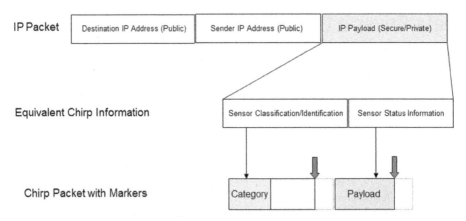

Figure 8-1. *An important distinction between chirp–based IoT packets and traditional IP is that the classification of the data type is part of the public and private markers of the chirp packet—easily "seen" and quickly acted upon by intermediate networking devices. By contrast, the only possible location for self-classification in IP packets is within the payload itself, which requires slower deep examination of the packet at intermediate hops*

The Ends are the Means

This book has described an emerging new architecture for the Internet of Things, designed to address the realities of connecting billions of relatively unsophisticated devices at the very edge of the network. The case has been made for a new terse self-classified protocol of chirps to be the communications medium to these devices, but there are currently no *commercially available* chirp end devices or chirp-enabled propagator nodes. The need for light, purpose-built protocols and devices is revolutionary, and these are early days.

An overnight replacement of existing IP networking protocols in the Internet of Things is impossible—and fortunately will not be required. As with most networking evolutions (twisted-pair Ethernet, Wi-Fi, and so on), the end points will eventually be the major numerical and technical drivers for change, and the support of both chirp and IP protocols to end devices side by side will be necessary to allow for network transformation. This will also be true for existing big data servers at the core of the nascent IoT: they cannot be changed out instantaneously. Fortunately, the propagator node architecture provides an ideal means for a gradual ("and") migration to take place, as described in detail here.

Many different organizations will play a role in the promulgation of the chirp-based Internet of Things. The suppliers of the thousands of types of end devices (from appliances to sensors to automobiles) will work with industry leaders in silicon integration and platform technology such as Intel Corporation to create integrated "chirp chips" in many different configurations and price points. Networking suppliers and home automation developers will build propagator nodes and also incorporate propagator node technology within existing types of equipment such as switches, routers, access points, set-top boxes, and more.

Carriers will make adaptations to the emerging chip-based architectures, many likely offering cloud-based services for interpreting and analyzing the small data flows from chirp streams, perhaps in combination with existing big data system suppliers. Large global Original Equipment Manufacturers (OEMs) will likely also be an important first class of customer and an early promoter of chirp-based protocols because they will be able to incorporate the technology end to end in their systems in parallel with the efforts of standards bodies and working groups, although these groups will most certainly play an important role in the long term.

Begin at the Edge

Fundamentally, the need for chirp-based protocols and the networking architecture to support them starts at the end device sensors and actuators that cannot use IPv6 for connectivity to the Internet of Things for the reasons of cost and complexity *and* that require self-classification that would be unwieldy in IP in any case. As described in Chapter 6, classification of these chirp–based end devices by type and function will take place via an extensible marker system carried within the chirp packet and will be easily visible as these packets transit the network.

Initially, the use of chirp classification categories could be proprietary or vendor-specific for an OEM supplying both the end devices and the integrator function/big data services, but the classifications will rapidly be formalized *across* organizations. (See more details of how these classifications could be created and managed in the following "Working in Groups" section). Once data streams are encoded in chirps with category classifications as to their type included, the data is inherently publish-ready, and some of the scaling benefits of the emerging IoT architecture can be seen.

CHIRPS IN IP PACKETS? WHY?

In advance of the proliferation of native chirp-based networks, the chirp information could also be specified within the payload section of a traditional IP packet by an "adapter" propagator node, which would encapsulate simpler terse data in the form of chirps with their inherent classification. This would allow subscribing big data systems to incorporate this information immediately and make possible a migration to the integrator function systems described in Chapter 5. The legacy IP packet containing chirp-formatted data will still need routing to reach a point-to-point destination, where the software is capable of deciphering the payload and acting on the data. That will likely be the first place where chirp protocols will be deployed.

The outgoing IP stream from the adapter propagator node could be Wi-Fi standards–based (i.e., 802.11). On the incoming chirp streams, the transceivers and their device drivers would need to look like ports on a local area network (LAN) switch for the Layer 2 hierarchical switch stack analogy to hold water. As long as the chirp device drivers on the adapter propagator node look and feel like IP "ports" on a legacy 802.11 access point (AP) "switch," multiple types of streams can be supported within the same AP. Alternately, network appliances may be installed to provide the chirp-to-IP interface, using Wi-Fi as a means to connect to the legacy IP network.

This technique provides one means of integrating chirp streams into legacy big data systems and may be an important transition path in the early days of chirp end devices. But it does not provide many of the other benefits of true chirp-based protocols such as broader data neighborhoods free of predefined IP peer-to-peer relationships and the tighter control loops made possible by distributing intelligence closer to the end devices in the form of publishing agents and localized integrator functions within propagator nodes. (Note that these limitations would be in place regardless of whether chirp protocols or IP are used.) The benefits of richer information usage and better control loops are much more attainable in native chirp networking and become even more compelling as the number of devices increases exponentially at the edge of the network.

In the long term, most propagator node/AP combinations will have support for native chirps and legacy IP built-in (see the following "Propagator Nodes Provide the 'And'" section), but other transitional APs could be imagined that provide powered USB sockets for device manufacturers to provide the chirp interface separately that are tuned for the specific chirp devices that they manufacture.

Making a Mark

In order to increase applicability of their end devices (and thus increase revenue), multiple suppliers of the same type of appliance, sensor, or actuator will be motivated to use the same formats in expressing their chirp data. It will thus be possible for their end devices to be incorporated across a broader range of integrator functions (from many suppliers) and in so doing, increase the number of potential applications.

Note that the chirp protocol uses both public and private sections, each with its own markers. Thus manufacturer-specific information and vendor-specific data can be safely represented within the same public category classifications. So although a marker of (for example) 6.8.11 might be used for a general category of moisture sensors, additional proprietary data within private segments of the chirps might specify vendor-specific features. In this form of incremental markers and meanings, a broad range of integrator functions provided by many different manufacturers and in support of different applications might add this moisture sensor chirp data stream to their information "neighborhood" and obtain some minimal data. This could take place even if the subscribing application was unknown to or even unthought-of by the organization originally deploying the moisture sensor.

But additional data might be included in a private section of the chirp, accessible only to integrator functions and other distributed intelligence in the network that possessed the correct "key." In our theoretical case, salinity or acidity might also be measured by the same sensor, but information on those parameters would be transported in proprietary private data segments within the same chirp packet as are the "generic" moisture readings.

Acting on Markers

Multiple intelligent agents may thus be acting on different strings within the chirp packet. The common propagator node operation may simply prune and bundle chirp streams into small data flows published to a wide variety of potential subscribers. Again, these subscribers may have the key to the proprietary additional data—or they may not.

In other specific propagator nodes, publishing agents may be biased by particular integrator functions to peer deeper into the private payload section and perform a more customized next level of routing and processing. This might include preferential routing to specific integrator function locations, "spoofing" by emulating round-trip acknowledgments locally, setting up specific forwarding bus timings or lower-level control loops, and so on.

Propagator Nodes Provide the "and"

In the early days, chirp-enabled devices will be the minority traffic on the Internet of Things. Simply because of the extensive installed base, large numbers of IP-equipped end devices will need to be accommodated as well. For that reason, many first-wave propagator node implementations will provide both chirp-ready *and* legacy IP connections such as Ethernet and Wi-Fi.

This emerging new class of hybrid devices will use chirp- and IP protocols interchangeably. These ambidextrous network elements will appear as two logically distinct devices, even if they are using the same transceivers (e.g., 2.4GHz unlicensed band radios). The added advantage of these IP-equipped devices is that they will also often have the processing power to house publishing agents, as required.

The input of these devices will be of three possible types as shown in Figure 8-2. Some IP packets will be the unmodified legacy IP streams from traditional devices. A second possible type (as noted in the sidebar "Chirps in IP Packets? Why?") will be encapsulated chirp streams within IP packets, intended for big data servers that are not yet fully chirp-aware. And a third class will be native emerging IoT architecture chirp data streams. This latter packet type will be intended specifically for chirp-aware integrator functions. Depending on the needs of the servers at the final destination, the transition propagator node will aggregate small data flows of chirp streams into IP packets or will simply pass them through legacy IP packets.

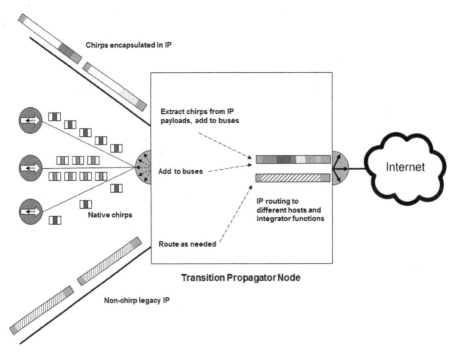

Figure 8-2. *Hybrid transition propagator nodes will handle legacy IP traffic, encapsulated chirp traffic, and native IoT chirps aggregated into small data streams*

As noted elsewhere, there will be many different packaging options for propagator nodes, including some with integrator functions on board that might handle some analysis and control tasks for their associated chirp end devices.

Because of their key role in translating and merging both legacy and emerging networks, transition propagator nodes of this type will necessarily be one of the first examples of equipment to be developed and marketed along with the first chirp-enabled end devices. Although some initial applications may be proprietary and OEM-vendor-specific, it is expected that more generic versions will also appear rapidly.

Open-Source Networking Solutions

One key to accelerating the development and proliferation of these translating generic propagator nodes will be taking full advantage of open-source technologies. One likely base (among a number of possibilities) upon which to build propagator node functions is OpenWrt, an operating system/embedded operating system based on the Linux kernel and primarily used on embedded devices to route network traffic. A chirp-enabled branch of this code could be produced quickly to allow rapid development of new propagator nodes, along with immediate integration into existing networking equipment operating under OpenWrt.

Gaining Access

Wi-Fi access points are one of the most numerous deployed networking solutions today, allowing a variety of devices equipped with 802.11 wireless capability to be connected into a network (today, nearly always IP-based). As such, they represent an attractive candidate for replacement by transition propagator nodes from a network topology standpoint. Virtually none of today's deployed APs supports the type of secure application layer and field upgradeability needed to incorporate chirp–enabled propagator node software directly.

But a new combined AP/propagator node device (likely based on OpenWrt) will include both traditional AP and IoT chirp–enabled propagator node capabilities, as seen in Figure 8-3. One key will be making the propagator node portion of the combined device "responsible" for both legacy and chirp communications to ensure that no changes are required for legacy IP IoT devices or big data servers. Multiple forms of connectivity will be made available over many different interfaces (e.g., Wi-Fi, IR, Bluetooth, Power Line, etc.).

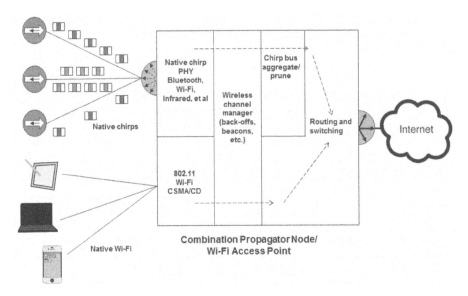

Figure 8-3. *Combination propagator node/AP devices will be an efficient means of merging traditional IP data with IoT chirp streams, sharing a single connection to the global Internet*

Clusters of simple chirp devices, currently not even imagined, will "connect" via these interfaces, with propagator nodes tasked to do the heavy lifting needed for conversion to small data streams, including routing and delivery via the logical "bus" described in Chapter 6. Much of this will occur without the need for arduous standards body consensus—at least initially (see the following "The Standards Conundrum" section). The chirp-enabled propagator nodes will integrate smoothly with existing IP devices and use the existing global Internet for transport. Even if chirp end devices use the same wireless frequencies as IP traffic (e.g., unlicensed bands), the propagator nodes will take over the timing and beaconing of all the wireless interfaces (both chirp-and IP-based), enforcing time slot reservations ensuring that chirp- and IP devices don't "speak" at the same time using existing capabilities within 802.11. Collaborative coexistence will be supported at all times within the emerging ecosystem because the propagator node/AP units are both chirp- and IP-aware.

It is hoped that using an open-source software model (see the previous discussion) for the development of propagator node capabilities may make it relatively straightforward for at least some existing AP manufacturers to quickly provide combined propagator node/AP units. These manufacturers would have the capability to extend the AP functionality to include an applications layer and also provide the device-layer abstractions so that new chirp devices can be supported with a "standard" interface to the chirp-to-IP bridge.

The Standards Conundrum

In the longer term, it is expected that a variety of standards bodies and working groups will formalize the specifics of the chirp packet and other elements of the emerging Internet of Things architecture. But the impending explosion in the growth of the IoT means that there is no time to wait for a drawn-out standard process before beginning to deploy this architecture. So a two-pronged approach will be necessary: de facto standards, working groups, and recommended practices allowing products to be brought to market quickly; along with a longer-term standards effort to codify these practices into standards. An example may be drawn from earlier machine-to-machine technology developments.

Machine-to-machine (M2M) communications are not new. Factory automation (e.g., robots, "intelligent" machines) has thrived on tight sensor–actuator control loops, where myriad sensors "feed" into Programmable Logic Controllers (PLCs) through the wired analog and digital I/O ports of the PLC controller. Relatively simple rule-based logic has been used to control complex machines composed of hundreds of sensors and actuators. The "circuits" turn on, based on logical switches turning on or off based on sensor data. When a circuit turns "on," actuators are activated. As a simple example, turning on a light switch closes a circuit to send electricity to a light bulb. Multiple such circuits, running concurrently within the PLC, have and do coordinate complex manufacturing processes.

These M2M communications and the tight control loops resulting from the custom-programmed circuits have clearly demonstrated the ability to generate complex competence from simple end devices such as sensors and actuators. Protocols and device drivers are often created by application software developers to meet the requirements of the specific process control required. A thriving manufacturing industry has evolved over the last two decades, based on proprietary, purpose-built, and terse sensor-actuator communications.

Standards existed for these sensors and actuators, but they were often home-grown by the sensor and actuator manufacturers, many times through Special Interest Groups (SIGs) within larger communities such as IEEE. However, because the device communications were local and entirely within a small community (e.g., a manufacturing line), there was no need for an overarching standard such as IP. In addition, in most cases the sensors/actuators are directly wired to the PLC controllers. There is no shared wireless spectrum to negotiate.

As more M2M sensors and actuators become wireless, sharing the same "air space" (i.e., unlicensed radio frequency spectrum) will become a challenge. Standard protocols such as ZigBee and Bluetooth evolved to support smaller communities of devices. However, all such devices were intended largely for human consumption of information and therefore were IP-based. They are currently being used to connect devices as part of a home audio system or home lighting system, being controlled by a home user's computer or smartphone. Note that they are human-in-the-loop systems; they are intended for humans to more conveniently control their environment, using the smartphone, for example, to remotely connect to their home lighting/heating systems or to link external keyboards or headphones to computers.

Machine-to-Machine Communications and Autonomy

More autonomous systems have evolved, where needed, to support more complex interactions from machine to machine and the machine with its environment. Although the human is still in the loop in a high-level control or advisory capacity, the devices are required to take more control in order to free up the human to do other tasks or because the human cannot respond adequately or in time (see Figure 7-3). This is exacerbated by the round-trip delays introduced in typical IP point-to-point relationships. By decoupling control loops, the emerging Internet of Things allows for rapid autonomous action near the edges of the network while still allowing long-term trends to be analyzed and overall control to take place at a higher level.

As described in earlier chapters, existing legacy protocols were originally intended for host-to-host or human-to-host conversations, not for the terse (and predominantly one-way) exchanges between myriad simple chirping end devices and big data integrator functions. But chirps will become the prevalent form of M2M communications in the IoT. Just as birds don't need to learn a common language to communicate effectively across the same medium (the air), so the end devices in the IoT may use only simple chirps optimized for their classification and function, counting on propagator nodes to make the conversions needed to allow use of the global Internet as the communications backbone.

It is simpler to delegate to these propagator nodes the task of performing translations across end device communities than to force everyone to use the same overly complex (and over-featured) legacy protocol formats. Overarching standards become less relevant as information neighborhoods become smarter at what they do within their areas of expertise. Autonomy and local control loops will also be much easier to operate and maintain without the IP overhead and round-trip communication necessary in legacy networks. This is another argument for simple and specialized chirp-based conversations between machines.

Shared Vocabularies and de facto Standards

In the machine-to-machine manufacturing application examples, the systems that currently use simplified communications schemes are generally private. In the emerging Internet of Things, publishing *and subscribing* to data streams is the primary activity, so obviously there is a critical need for shared vocabularies. A simple *but open* scheme, such as chirp-based networking, provides the potential for tremendous economies of scale in place of private vocabularies.

Networking standards such as IP were based on communication protocols at the lower level of routing and networking without specifying payload vocabularies. As long as the IP packet headers were universally understood, the payload portion of the packet would be routed correctly to the requested destination. The contents of the payload were decipherable by the recipient at the destination address; everything else served primarily as indicators of a routing infrastructure.

Because many agents will be performing similar tasks, shared networking techniques and payload vocabularies within application segments (e.g., moisture sensors) will engender reusability of data. Thus major OEMS such as General Electric, Samsung, Siemens, and Honeywell (among many others) may cooperate on the chirp protocol for products that overlap in functionality as a first level of interoperability.

This cooperation may also extend to some common functionality between OEMs in the publishing agent resident on some classes of propagator nodes. Although it would require a great deal of coordinated collaboration, it also would reduce the overall complexity of the system. Because the publishers and subscribers for similar devices will share common interests, there is value in sharing the same computing resources resident on the propagator nodes.

Propagator nodes are operating close to the edge of the network, so using the same publishing agents makes things simpler. Through the common vocabulary of similar devices, a new form of standards will emerge: one that is more focused on communicating state information versus networking/routing flow. Hegemonies exist within application segments in which collaboration is implicit. For example, the same repair centers service multiple types of home appliances (e.g., washing machines) from competing brands, or multiple pieces of different equipment at one site (see Figure 8-4). Providing the same vocabulary for diagnostics would make it simpler for a repair staffer to do the work.

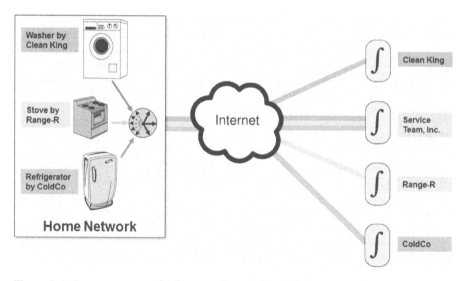

Figure 8-4. *In some cases, multiple networks may share information and network elements. Here, three types of machines from different manufacturers report usage and trends to independent integrator functions for each manufacturer, but they share status and alarm reports to a common third-party service company*

In time, sophisticated combined subsystems of analysis and control may develop organically near the edge of the network. These systems of systems, each capable of functioning autonomously, will increasingly continue to do so. Humans will be in the loop only for analysis of trends or periodic tuning and tweaking.

Build it and End Devices will Come

The explosion of smart devices (e.g., smartphones, home automation products) occurred because the support infrastructure was both prevalent and inexpensive. Internet connectivity became ubiquitous, at least in developed countries. This ready Internet access connected the lower-level consumer products to the higher end of cloud services and their applications.

A three-tiered ecosystem emerged: at the top, cloud-based applications could be downloaded to devices (computers and smartphones) via the middle layer of Internet connectivity, performed by an expanding network support infrastructure. Devices were thus "connected" to the cloud. New devices such as the Apple iPod were conceivable, in which the heavy lifting was performed by an intermediary computer connected to cloud applications. Some (agents, for example) could also run locally on the computer. In terms of the end device/propagator node/integrator function model of the IoT, end devices can similarly become widespread quickly when the network is there to support them.

In terms of a three-layered framework, at least two of three pieces must be available because only then would the cost of developing the third piece become economically viable. For example, iPods, with their limited inherent communications functionality (i.e., no IP stack), could not exist if computers running iTunes software did not exist as an intermediary or if the global Internet did not exist as a connection to cloud-based music services. In that framework, the "end device" (iPod) was supported by computer software downloaded to computers (propagator nodes within the IoT) connected to the cloud-based services via the Internet (the IoT's integrator functions).

OEM Leverage

In the legacy concept of the Internet of Things, IP is needed at each point (end device, networking element, and server). But for a chirp-based IoT to develop and proliferate, some use must be made of the existing elements to avoid the cost, complexity, and elapsed time necessary for a complete ground-up build-out.

OEM manufacturers are a likely first place where chirp-based disruptions would occur. OEMs are typically not interested in providing networking infrastructure, but their highest-end products (e.g., refrigerators, TVs) are becoming connected via IP. There is enough computing horsepower in these products to potentially serve as chirp-based propagator nodes for the OEM's large number of simpler, more lightweight devices that will never justify IP. The higher-cost devices would therefore support their less-sophisticated, chirp-based "country cousins."

There is incentive, therefore, to purchase a GE toaster if one owns a GE refrigerator, without burdening the toaster with its own IP connectivity. Or the presence of a Samsung TV would ensure that other Samsung devices, using low cost infrared transceivers (as in the TV remote), would coexist as part of the home entertainment system without each component requiring its own IP connectivity.

The "two-out-of-three" model makes sense for both manufacturers and consumers, as shown in Figure 8-5. Consumers pay less for their low-end devices (toasters) and their connectivity. Manufacturers can leverage their brands to provide interoperable families of products, all of which are connected in some fashion. In later years, they might potentially be updated via downloadable software to service chirp-based devices. And if desired, OEM manufacturers could use private markers and payloads in the chirp streams to lock-in buyers—although there will also be incentives to make public some or all of the information.

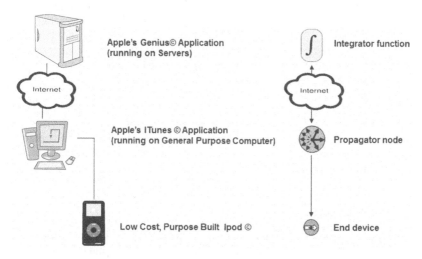

Figure 8-5. *Like a downloadable media player that is only economically viable if cost-effective computing power and global connectivity are already present, so an OEM's installed IP device and the global Internet might enable new low–cost end devices*

Applications-developer communities similar to Apple and Android application marketplaces will be encouraged to provide new applications for these newly connected devices. Ecosystems will emerge in which smarter IP-based products support their simpler chirp-enabled products. Giving away a free chirp-enabled toaster with every refrigerator purchase begins to make sense—the toaster becomes a useful device for control by the 'fridge. In this case, the refrigerator is the computer running applications on behalf of the toaster, which is still a purpose-built device. This mirrors the case of iTunes on a computer managing the simpler iPod in a previous generation of the three-layered ecosystem.

Shared Software and Business Process Vocabularies

Linux and its variants have become established as a primary embedded–system operating environment, largely due to open software initiatives. Proof-of-concept propagator nodes and publishing agents now being developed are currently based on Linux variants, and many future implementations will likely follow suit.

In the enterprise business world, Java is widely used for programming applications that may be written once and (theoretically, at least) used in many places. Programming in Java is simpler and more enterprise-business-process friendly. Translation mechanisms will evolve to convert business processes originally expressed in visual programming languages or in Java to simple rules that will be downloaded to integrator functions and/or the publishing agents on the propagator nodes. And this will be true for other enterprise software, as well.

Software as a Service (SaaS) has become a staple in cloud-based computing, and its counterpart in the Internet of Things may be a set of functions to be loaded on propagator nodes. Multiple propagator nodes from diverse manufacturers will need to connect and support a variety of big data services, so it is likely that the means to do so, including the translation mechanisms, will be made available as open source. Large enterprises and OEMs may use customized versions with proprietary protocols to access the private section of chirp protocols, but the ecosystem will support common vocabularies and processes to a large degree. Hence the semantics of an operation will be understood by the same category of devices, regardless of their brand.

The need to communicate in the same manner to big data cloud servers will drive common APIs and high-level control languages, as in the case of shared vocabularies. Although standards may emerge for these vocabularies in the long term, OEMS, working groups, and special interest groups will continue to promote this collaboration, driven by mutual interests and common practices.

Working in Groups

All in all, an organic process is expected for the development and deployment of the emerging Internet of Things architecture. But certain basic structures and tenants are keys to the success of the IoT. It is especially critical that the basic chirp structure be agreed upon and top-level classifications defined by a critical mass of IoT constituent organizations. The goal would be to reach a consensus rapidly on crucial parameters, permitting many companies and organizations to move quickly to develop their own products.

There are multiple alternate paths this development might take. One successful model is that followed by Bluetooth technology, which essentially began as a development within one company, but was shepherded by a handful of large companies collaborating as a special interest group. The time for successful interoperability testing and adoption of the technology was measured in years, however. The author favors a potentially more rapid approach, based on the open-source model (as seen with the OpenWrt distribution for Linux-based networking).

Whatever direction the initial development takes, the primary task will be definition of the highest levels of the chirp marker classification structure. It is anticipated that a one-byte first-order classification will provide a sufficient starting point for later added granularity. With these roughly 255 end-device categories set, working groups oriented toward specific industries could further define lower levels of addressing granularity. (Recall that the chirp marker structure is extensible to a very large numbers of classifications encompassing future needs.)

After the basics of the IoT are described, and products based on early versions of the definitions and parameters are being offered, it is likely that some standards body, such as the IEEE, will adopt chirp technologies into an existing standard as a working group or initiate a new standards effort. This would likely be driven by a larger player or OEM wishing to embrace standardization.

The rapidly expanding number of Internet of Things devices will create the need for this emerging technology in short order, so approaches that require minimum time to fruition are desirable.

Call to Constituencies for the IoT

Many different kinds of organization will have a stake in the success of the emerging Internet of Things. This section briefly describes what steps will be required of each of these constituencies.

Semiconductor Providers

Integrated Circuit (IC) "chirp chips" will be necessary for reasons of cost and power consumption at the end devices. Because of the minimal hardware and memory demands of the chirp protocol, the initial versions of these ICs may also be relatively simple, with greater integration, lower cost, and lower power consumption coming over time.

For propagator nodes, many off-the-shelf System-on-a-Chip (SoC) and System-in-a-Package solutions designed for data processing and network interfaces for traditional networking devices may be useful as building blocks, along with additional specialized ICs for the chirp "side" of the devices. For smaller packages in which publishing agents or integrator functions are incorporated, emerging compact devices such as Intel's Quark SoC may be preferred. Integrator functions will usually operate on general-purpose processors, and filter gateways may use existing router hardware.

The key challenge for semiconductor providers will be a quick determination of the specific parameters of the chirp protocol to allow rapid development. It is hoped that one or more semiconductor vendors will participate in early working groups and special interest groups.

Appliance and Other End Device Manufacturers

A number of sensor, actuator, and appliance manufacturers have already incorporated IP protocol stacks into their more sophisticated Internet of Things products. For these products, incorporating chirp self-classified data formats within IP payloads as an interim step toward the emerging IoT architecture may be a matter of software revision only. But the vast majority of end device types that will eventually be connected to the IoT do not yet have *any* network interface.

For these devices, the problem is somewhat chicken-and-egg: they will likely not be able to cost-effectively move forward until IC chirp chips are available for specific applications; and the semiconductor manufacturers may not move ahead rapidly with optimized chirp chips until the end devices are being developed. As noted in

"Major End-to-End OEMs" below, OEMs with a vested interest in end-to-end systems may develop the first wave of end devices with native chirp protocols, which may serve to accelerate broader deployment.

On the plus side, because the chirp protocol requires no central registry of network addresses (as the MAC IDs needed for Ethernet, 802.11, Bluetooth, and others), end device manufacturers may move quickly and independently to adopt chirp technology. Working from published top-level device-type classifications and the overall chirp packet structure, they may easily build devices that will interoperate with propagator nodes and integrator functions built by others.

Networking Equipment Vendors

Because the technology requirements are very similar, many of today's leading networking equipment vendors may move directly into the propagator node business. The only challenge may be philosophical rather than technical: a willingness to give up the mantra of "IPv6 everywhere" for the Internet of Things. The benefit, of course, is access to the new market to connect hundreds of billions of new devices. "Greenfield" markets are often more profitable than ongoing commoditizing sectors, so this alone may provide ample justification for investment.

But even vendors who steadfastly remain in the IP-only camp will still find their products used in expansions of the global Internet infrastructure needed between propagator nodes and integrator functions. Upon reaching the Internet, packets are packets – and the rising tide of the IoT will lift many boats. Existing IPv6 router devices may also be a good basis for the IoT filter gateways needed in some applications. In many cases, only configuration and programming will be needed.

Home Automation/Entertainment Suppliers

A tremendous potential exists for expansion of home networking in the form of chirp-enabled networking. One focus may be the TV set-top box (or a smart TV) that already increasingly includes Internet access. One can imagine future devices that connect not only to existing home equipment via infrared interfaces and the Internet via cable or Wi-Fi but also link the rest of the devices in the home via Power Line, Wi-Fi, or other technologies. Alternately, combination home propagator node/APs with the appropriate chirp transceivers built in will support both Wi-Fi IP and chirp traffic.

A local integrator function within the propagator node could provide the "brains" for home entertainment, climate control, security, energy management, and so on. Because this device will have access to a much broader set of devices *as well as other data sources* such as weather reports and utility updates, it will optimize the operation of the home as not previously possible. Unlike expensive proprietary solutions offered to date, proliferation of compatible chirp-enabled products will reduce costs, allow expansion over time, and eliminate reliance on single-vendor offerings.

Coordination with nascent standards work in the home automation space, and some integration or translation of existing open- or quasi-open-source technologies such as C-Bus, Insteon, KNX, X10, and ZigBee, will likely be important to acceptance of chirp-based end devices in the home.

Carriers and Big Data Providers

At the most basic level, major carriers will need to do nothing to support traffic from the emerging Internet of Things. Beyond the IP-equipped propagator nodes, traffic will be identical to all other Internet traffic and can be carried via the same backbone infrastructure. But there will be tremendous opportunities for cloud-based integrator functions, whether simply in the form of "power-by-the-hour" servers or value-added analysis and control services. The classification-based chirp protocol allows for preferential routing of specific small data flows, if desired.

Similarly, today's big data providers may integrate small data flows emanating from aggregated chirp data streams relatively straightforwardly with today's equipment and architectures. Big data customer optimization and the opportunity for new enhanced services will come as more propagator nodes are deployed that include on-board publishing agents. As big data providers move to the integrator function model for data analysis and control, they will be able to "bias" the distributed publishing agents (refer to Chapter 5) to allow independent local control loops for autonomous functions, as well as to tune the type, amount, and frequency of data being forwarded.

Major End-to-End OEMs

As mentioned earlier, one of the ways that long standardization cycles may be avoided in the implementation of the chirp-enabled Internet of Things is through the actions of large global Original Equipment Manufacturers (OEMs). Many of these OEMS already deliver solutions that reach from the edges of the enterprise or home to large centralized organizations. In many applications, these OEMs already use IP-powered networks extended by the global Internet to reach far-flung end devices, although data structures within the IP payload may be proprietary. But the emerging chirp-enabled architecture for the Internet of Things will benefit these OEMs in two ways.

The first and perhaps most obvious is that the cost (for processing, memory, power, and management) will be much lower for chirp-enabled end devices than for IP-enabled end devices. This cost savings will allow many more types and classes of equipment to be brought into the network, in which they may be monitored or controlled by the OEM systems. This extends the reach and differentiates lower-end equipment from generic competitors.

The second benefit is especially unique to the self-classified chirp traffic characteristic of the IoT: the capability to seek out and recruit *non-proprietary* data streams into an information neighborhood to provide added value to the OEM customer. The story is told of a global OEM that delivered a large robotic precision assembly system to India and set the machine up precisely as had been done in other parts of the world. Performance was poor with many breakdowns.

Eventually, an on-site engineer recognized that the higher ambient temperature was causing a deterioration of the low-viscosity lubricant called for in the manufacturer's specs developed in cooler climates. When this lubricant was replaced with a version more suitable for the environment, the equipment operated reliably. In earlier times, this sort of observation required an on-site human to make the observation and analysis.

But in the new world of the Internet of Things, the OEM might be able to recruit chirp data streams from existing nearby sensors that would provide temperature, humidity, or other parameters that would help diagnose a fault condition at a distant installation. Because of the self-classified chirp protocol, these sensors could be installed by anyone, not necessarily the OEM. Unplanned and previously unknown data sources may be exploited along with data from the OEM's own equipment for a better experience for the end customer (refer to Figure 7-4).

Global Scope, Vast Numbers, Constant Adaptation, New Insights

As many have suggested in the past, it would certainly be *theoretically* possible for the Internet of Things to remain on traditional protocols such as IPv6. But for all the reasons described in this book, that path would close off the unprecedented potential of the Internet of Things. The scope is simply too large and the costs too great to expect traditional protocols to meet the need. Delaying deployment of a new architecture is no solution because it will never be possible to catch up.

The emerging Internet of Things architecture is designed to manage the unprecedented coming tsunami of data flowing to-and-from billions of end devices for applications both mundane and innovative. Lightweight self-identified protocols at the edge of the network, distributed networking intelligence, and ever-learning analysis and control functions will deliver on the promise of the IoT. Far from merely *addressing* billions of end points, this new architecture enables them to provide the information needed for powerful new knowledge, control, and efficiency in the final phase of the evolution of the Internet.

Index

Get the eBook for only $10!

> Now you can take the weightless companion with you anywhere, anytime. Your purchase of this book entitles you to 3 electronic versions for only $10.

This Apress title will prove so indispensible that you'll want to carry it with you everywhere, which is why we are offering the eBook in 3 formats for only $10 if you have already purchased the print book.

Convenient and fully searchable, the PDF version enables you to easily find and copy code—or perform examples by quickly toggling between instructions and   applications. The MOBI format is ideal for your Kindle, while the ePUB can be utilized on a variety of mobile devices.

Go to www.apress.com/promo/tendollars to purchase your companion eBook.

Lightning Source UK Ltd.
Milton Keynes UK
UKHW01f0933130618
324162UK00001B/77/P